# JESUS —IS— GOD

*Understanding How You Get to Heaven*

Leonard Horn

ISBN 979-8-89309-723-8 (Paperback)
ISBN 979-8-89309-724-5 (Digital)

Copyright © 2024 Leonard Horn
All rights reserved
First Edition

All rights reserved. No part of this publication may be reproduced, distributed, or transmitted in any form or by any means, including photocopying, recording, or other electronic or mechanical methods without the prior written permission of the publisher. For permission requests, solicit the publisher via the address below.

Covenant Books
11661 Hwy 707
Murrells Inlet, SC 29576
www.covenantbooks.com

# CONTENTS

Introduction ..................................................................v

Chapter 1: Who Is Jesus and Why Is He God? ...........................1
Chapter 2: Evidence of Jesus Deity from the Old and
New Testaments......................................................4
Chapter 3: Eyewitness Accounts about Jesus Being God ..............8
Chapter 4: My Misconceptions about Jesus before I
Learned about the True Jesus of the Bible
and the Trinity........................................................18
Chapter 5: What Is the Meaning of the Trinity .........................30
Chapter 6: Christians: Who Are They and What Do
Christians Have to Do with Jesus? ..........................34
Chapter 7: Scriptures on God the Father .................................47
Chapter 8: God the Son (Jesus): The Teachings of Jesus ............52
Chapter 9: Scripture References about God the Holy Spirit .....139
Chapter 10: Jesus Is GOD throughout the Bible with Key
Scriptures That Show He Is GOD ..........................160
Chapter 11: Scriptures That Feature All Three Persons of GOD.....170
Chapter 12: Key Bible Scriptures about Jesus Being GOD ..........176
Chapter 13: Why Is Jesus So Important and Vital for
Every Nation and All People...................................189
Chapter 14: Scriptures on Salvation .........................................208
Chapter 15: The Summary of Why Jesus Is GOD ......................219
Chapter 16: Thank You..........................................................224

# INTRODUCTION

The reason for this book is to hopefully inform all nations of the importance of Jesus Christ to the world.

In a courtroom case, the objective is to prove, or disprove, a person's guilt or innocence. The reason I am using this example is because most people in the world understand the concept of court procedures. By using the New King James Version (NKJV), which shows many eyewitness accounts of Jesus's time here on earth, I hope to establish concrete proof that Jesus is God.

Throughout this book, I'm going to limit my commentary about the scriptures that I present as evidence in an effort to let the Word of God shine, as Hebrews 4:12 the Word of God says, "For the word of God is living and powerful, and sharper than any two-edged sword, piercing even to the division soul and spirit, and of the thoughts and intents of the heart." And that says it all.

I would like to thank all of the readers in advance for your time and trust in the information I have given you. God bless you all, in Jesus's name.

Let's start with a word of prayer:

> Heavenly Father, I ask that You give me the words to say based on Your Words in the Bible (NKJV). Please allow every reader to receive the understanding and the truth of your word, in Jesus's name. Amen.

# CHAPTER 1

## Who Is Jesus and Why Is He God?

Jesus is God. If we take a look at the Gospel of John in the Bible (NKJV), specifically John 20:30–31, it says, "And truly Jesus did many other signs in the presence of His disciples, which are not written in this book; but these are written that you may believe that Jesus is the Christ, the Christ, the Son of God, and that believing you may have life in His name."

John was one of Jesus's original twelve disciples, also one of three closest to Jesus. In fact John would refer to himself as "the one that Jesus loved." John also wrote four other books that are recorded in the Bible. In addition to St. John, there are 1 John, 2 John, 3 John, and the Revelation.

The apostle John proves that Jesus is God by the multiple "I Am" statements that Jesus made, which is based on the Old Testament. In Exodus 3:14, it says, "And God said to Moses, '*I Am Who I am*.' And He said, 'Thus you shall say to the children of Israel, "I Am has sent me to you."'"

There are multiple scriptures in St. John that shows Jesus's "I Am" statements.

1) John 6:48–50 says, "I Am the bread of life. Your fathers ate the manna in the wilderness, and are dead. This is the

bread which comes down from heaven, that one may eat of it and not die."

Here's another "I Am" statement of Jesus indicating that He is God:

2) John 8:23 says, "And He said to them, 'You are from beneath; I am from above. You are of this world; I am not of this world.'"

Here's another "I Am" statement that Jesus made professing who He is:

3) John 8:12 says, "Then Jesus spoke to them again, saying, 'I am the light of the world. He who follows Me shall not walk in darkness, but have the light of life.'"

Here's another "I Am" statement Jesus made describing His status:

4) John 10:9 says, "I Am the door. If anyone enters by Me, he will be saved, and will go in and out and find pasture."

Here's another "I Am statement" Jesus made:

5) John 10:10 (KJV) says, "The thief does not come except to steal, and to kill, and to destroy. I Am come that they may have life, and that they may have it more abundantly."

Here's another "I Am" statement Jesus made that shows who He is:

6) John 10:11 says, "I Am the good shepherd. The good shepherd gives His life for the sheep."

Here's another "I Am" statement Jesus made, establishing evidence that He is God:

7) John 11:25–26 says, "Jesus said to her, 'I am the resurrection and the life. He who believes in Me, thought he may die, he shall live. And whoever lives and believes in Me shall never die. Do you believe this?'"

Here's another "I Am" statement Jesus made, even further proving that He is God:

8) John 14:6 says, "Jesus said to him, "I Am the way, truth, and the life. No one comes to the Father except through Me.'"

Here's another "I Am" statement Jesus made:

9) John 18:6 says, "Now when He said to them, 'I am He.' They drew back and fell to the ground."

   I saved this scripture for last because it ties into the first scripture I showed you in the beginning of Jesus's "I Am" statements. The first "I Am" statement came from *Exodus 3:14* in the Old Testament when God said to Moses "I Am that I Am."

   This "I Am" statement that Jesus made came from the book of John: John 8:58 says, "Jesus said to them, 'Most assuredly, I say to you, before Abraham was, I Am.'"

This proves, from Jesus's own words, that He is God.

"I Am" means Yhwh (Yahweh), the Self-Existing One. *Merriam Webster* defines the word *Yahweh*: (noun) God used especially by the ancient Hebrews. The synonyms are *Almighty, Creator, God Everlasting, Father, King, Eternal, Maker, Supreme Being, Author, Deity, Lord, Divinity,* and *Godhead*.

In the following chapters, I'll share more verses to help you understand the fact of Jesus being God and hopefully unfold more revelation on who Jesus is and His importance to *all* of our lives.

# CHAPTER 2

## Evidence of Jesus Deity from the Old and New Testaments

Now let's take a look at scripture references about Jesus deity from the Old and New Testaments in a side-by-side manner.

I highly encourage *all* readers of this book to use this book only as a reference pointing you to Jesus. A fuller understanding of who Jesus is can only be found in the pages of God's Word, the Bible. The Bible is God speaking to you.

### Scriptures from Old and New Testament

Continuing on from the "I Am" statements in chapter 1 on what God told Moses: "I Am that I Am."

*New Testament*

> Your father Abraham rejoiced to see My day, and he saw it and was glad. The Jews said to Him, "You are not yet fifty years old, and You seen Abraham?" Jesus said to them, "Most assuredly, I say to you, before Abraham was I Am." (John 8:56)

*Old Testament*

> Then Moses said to God, "Indeed, when I come to the children of Israel and say to them, 'The God of your fathers has sent me to you,' and they say to me, 'What is His name?' What shall I say to them?" And God said to Moses, "I AM WHO I AM." And He said, "Thus you shall say to the children of Israel, 'I AM has sent you.'" Moreover, God said to Moses, "Thus you shall say to the children of Israel: 'The Lord God of your fathers, the God of Abraham, the God of Isaac, and the God of Jacob, has sent me to you. This is My name forever, and this is My memorial to all generation.'" (Exodus 3:13–15)

*New Testament*

> And she will bring forth a Son, and you shall call His name Jesus, for He will save His people from their sins. Behold, the virgin shall be with child, and bear a Son and they shall call His name Immanuel which is translated "God with us" and did not know her till she had brought forth her firstborn Son. And called His name Jesus. (Matthew 1:21, 23, 25)

*Old Testament*

> Therefore the Lord Himself will give you a sign: Behold, the virgin shall conceive and bear a Son, and shall call His name Immanuel. (Isaiah 7:14)

*New Testament*

> In whom we have redemption through his blood, the forgiveness of sins. He is the image of the invisible God, the first born over all creation. For by Him all things were created that are in heaven and that are on earth, visible and invisible, whether thrones or dominions or principalities or powers. All things were created through Him and for Him. (Colossians 1:14–17)

*Old Testament*

> In the beginning God created the heavens and the earth. (Genesis 1:1)

*New Testament*

> In the beginning was the Word, and the Word was God. He was in the beginning with God All things were made through Him, and without Him nothing was made that was made. (John 1:1–3)

> And the Word was made flesh, and dwelt among us, and we beheld His glory, the glory as of the only begotten of the Father full of grace and truth. (John 1:14 KJV)

*Old Testament*

> For who is God, except the Lord? And who is a rock, except our God?
> The Lord lives! Blessed be my Rock! Let the God of my salvation be exalted. (Psalm 18:31 and 46)

*New Testament*

> I, Jesus, have sent My angel to testify to you these things in the churches. I am the Root and Offspring of David, the Bright and Morning Star. (Revelation 22:16)

# CHAPTER 3

## Eyewitness Accounts about Jesus Being God

There are many scriptures that testify and witness to the accounts of Jesus. Some are duplicated in the Gospels of Matthew, Mark, Luke, and John in the New Testament of the Bible. In this book, at minimum, I've scratched the surface. Once again, I encourage all readers of this book to please study the Bible from Genesis through Revelation.

I'll start this section with what the Bible says in 2 Peter 1:16–18:

> For we did not follow cunningly devised fables when we made known to you the power and coming of our Lord Jesus Christ, but were eyewitness of His majesty. For He received from God the Father honor and glory when such a voice came to Him from the Excellent Glory: "This is My beloved Son, in whom I am well pleased." And we heard this voice which came from heaven when we were with Him on the holy mountain.

What these verses of Scripture are showing, as it relates to Jesus being God, is that God the Father spoke to Jesus, His Son, while

Jesus was on earth and the disciples heard what God the Father said from heaven to God the Son (Jesus) here on earth.

Now let's continue to view other scriptures from the Bible that prove that Jesus is God. Using witness-reference scriptures gives us a more full and better understanding of this concept. Again, I urge all readers to look them all up in the King James Version Bible or for a little easier read, use the NKJV.

Luke 24:25–47 says,

> Then He said to them, "O foolish ones, and slow of heart to believe in all that the prophets have spoken! Ought not the Christ to have suffered these things and to enter in His glory?" And beginning at Moses and all the Prophets, He expounded to them in all the Scriptures the things concerning Himself. Then they drew near to the village where they were going, and He indicated that He would have gone farther. But they constrained Him saying, "Abide with us, for it is toward evening, and the day is far spent." And He went in to stay with them. Now it came to pass, as He sat at the table with them, that He took bread, blessed and broke it, and gave it to them. Then their eyes were opened and they knew Him: and He vanished from their sight. And they said to one another, "Did not our heart burn within us while He talked with us on the road, and while He opened the Scriptures to us?" So they rose up that very hour and returned to Jerusalem and found the eleven and those who were with them gathered together, saying, "The Lord is risen indeed and has appeared to Simon!" And they told about the things that had happened on the road and how He was known to them in the breaking of bread. Now as they said these things, Jesus Himself stood in the midst of

them and said to them, "Peace to you" But they were terrified and frightened and supposed they had seen a spirit. And He said to them, "Why are you troubled? And why do doubts arise in your hearts? Behold My hands and My feet, that is I Myself. Handle Me and see, for a spirit does not have flesh and bones as you see I have." When He had said this, He showed them His hands and His feet. But while they still did not believe for joy, and marveled, He said to them, "Have you any food here?" So they gave Him a piece of a broiled fish and some honeycomb. And He took it and ate in their presence. Then He said to them, "These are the words which I spoke to you while I was still with you that all things must be fulfilled which were written in the Law of Moses and the Prophets and the Psalms concerning Me." And He opened their understanding that they might comprehend the Scriptures. Then He said to them, "Thus it is written, and thus it was necessary for the Christ to suffer and to rise from the dead the third day. And that repentance and remission of sins should be preached in His name to all nations, beginning at Jerusalem. And you are witness of these things."

What I'd like for you to notice here is that, after Jesus's resurrection from the dead, He spoke to two of the disciples, but they did not recognize Him. In verse 31, the Bible speaks of Jesus vanishing out of their sight. Jesus disappeared. Regular people don't just vanish. My mission here, and through this book, is to show you that Jesus is GOD. In verse 48, Jesus said, "And you are witness these things." In various scripture passages, the Bible reveals of Jesus coming from heaven to earth, which we will explore more as we dive deeper into this book.

JESUS IS GOD

This witness was John the Baptist, Jesus's cousin, the son of Zechariah and Elizabeth. This scripture speak of Jesus.

John 1:6–18 says,

> There was man sent from God, whose name was John. This man came for a witness, to bear witness of the Light, that all through him might believe. He was not that Light, but was sent to bear witness of that Light. That was the true Light which gives light to every man coming into the world. He was in the world, and the world was made through Him. He came to His own, and His own did not receive Him. But as many as received Him, to them He gave the right to become children of God, to those who believe in His name: who were born, not of blood, nor of the will of the flesh, nor of the will of man, but of God. And the Word became flesh and dwelt among us, and we beheld His glory, the glory as of the only begotten of the Father, full of grace and truth. John bore witness of Him and cried out, saying, "This was He of whom I said, 'He who comes after me is preferred before me, for He was before me.'" And of His fullness we have all received, and grace for grace. For the law was given through Moses, but grace and truth came through Jesus Christ. No one has seen God at any time. The only begotten Son, who is in the bosom of the Father, He has declared Him.

Jesus said to a multitude of witnesses as He taught on a mountain,

> You are the light of the world. A city that is set on a hill cannot be hidden. Nor do they light a lamp and put it under a basket, but on a

> lamp stand, and it gives light to all who are in the house. Let your light so shine before men, that they may see your good works and glorify your Father in heaven. (Matthew 5:14–16)

Revelation 21:22–23 says,

> But I saw no temple in it, for the Lord God Almighty and the Lamb are its temple. The city had no need of the sun or of the moon to shine in it, for the glory of God illuminated it. The Lamb is its light.

This last passage of scripture speaks of the Lamb, who is Jesus, along with God the Father, the Almighty, Who is in heaven, being the Light of heaven and that there is no need anymore of the sun or the moon, which normally gives light to humans here on earth.

> The next day John saw Jesus coming towards him and said, "Behold! The Lamb of God who takes away the sin of the world! This is He of whom I said, 'After me comes a Man who is preferred before me, for He was before me.' I did not know Him; but that He should be revealed to Israel, therefore I came baptizing with water." And John bore witness, saying, "I saw the Spirit descending from heaven like a dove, and He remained upon Him." (John 1:29–32)

> In those days, John the Baptist came preaching in the wilderness of Judea, and saying, "Repent for the kingdom of heaven is at hand!" For this is he who was spoken of by the prophet Isaiah, saying: "The voice of one crying in the wilderness: 'Prepare the way of the Lord; Make His paths straight.'" (Matthew 3:1–3)

And now this account of John the Baptist preaching about Jesus's coming into the world. John 1:39 says,

> He said to them, "Come and see." They came and saw where He was staying, and remained with Him that day (now it was about the tenth hour). One of the two who heard John speak, and followed Him, was Andrew, Simon Peter's brother. He first found his own brother Simon, and said to him, "We have found the Messiah" (which is translated, the Christ, which means Anointed One).

The Messiah is the promised and expected deliverer of the Jewish people from God in heaven. The Anointed One is Jesus Christ.

Hebrews 12:1–2 says,

> Therefore, we also, since we are surrounded by so great a cloud of witnesses, let us lay aside every weight, and the sin which so easily ensnares us, and let us run with endurance the race that is set before us, looking unto Jesus, the author and finisher of our faith, who for the joy that was set before Him endured the cross, despising the shame, and has sat down at the right hand of the throne of God.

In these two scripture passages, there are so many great subject matters that could be pointed out that would be a blessing. Look at the end of verse 2 where it says, "And has sat down at the right hand of the throne of God." This shows that Jesus is back in Heaven from earth.

These scriptures are all bits of proofs that Jesus is God.

Let's continue viewing the testimonies and witnesses of Jesus Christ.

John 5:31–36 says,

> (Jesus speaking) If I bear witness of myself, My witness is not true. There is another who bears witness of Me, and I know that the witness which He witnesses of Me is true. You have sent to John, and he has borne witness to the truth. Yet I do not receive testimony from man, but I say these things that you may be saved. He was the burning and shining lamp, and you were willing for a time to rejoice in his light. But I have a greater witness than John's; for the works which the Father has given Me to finish—the very works that I do—bear witness of Me, that the Father's sent Me.

Please keep in mind that the Father that Jesus speaks of is God the Father, and He is in heaven. There will be more clarity on this later. Let's continue.

> Now when they had fulfilled all that was written concerning Him, they took Him down from the tree and laid Him in a tomb. But God raised Him from the dead. He was seen for many days by those who came up with Him from Galilee to Jerusalem, who are His witnesses to the people. (Acts 13:29–31)

> While thus occupied, as I journey to Damascus with authority and commission from the chief priests, at midday, O king, along the road I saw a light from heaven, brighter than the sun, shining around me and those who journeyed with me. And when we all had fallen to the ground, I heard a voice speaking to me and saying in the Hebrew language, "Saul, Saul, why are you

> persecuting Me? It is hard for you to kick against the goads." So I said, "Who are You, Lord?" And He said, "I am Jesus, whom you are persecuting. But rise and stand on your feet; for I have appeared to you for this purpose, to make you a minister and a witness both of the things which you have seen and of the things which I will yet reveal to you. I will deliver you from the Jewish people, as well as from the Gentiles, to whom I now send you, to open their eyes, in order to turn them from darkness to light, and from the power of satan to God, that they may receive forgiveness of sins and an inheritance among those who are sanctified by faith in Me." (Acts 26:12–15)

These scriptures speak about Jesus having already ascended to heaven; and at the time, Saul, who later was renamed Paul, was persecuting believers in Christ Jesus. Saul was on his way to Damascus to attempt to continue his persecution of Jesus's followers when this event happened to him. The point of this is in verse 15. Saul asked, "Who are You, Lord?" And He said "I am Jesus, whom you are persecuting."

Matthew 17:1–9 says,

> Now after six days Jesus took Peter, James, and John his brother, Led them up on a high mountain by themselves; and He was transfigure before them. His face shone like the sun, and His clothes became as white as the light. And behold, Moses and Elijah appeared to them, talking with Him. Then Peter answered and said to Jesus, "Lord it is good for us to be here; if You wish, let us make here three tabernacles: one for You, one for Moses, and one for Elijah." While he was still speaking, behold, a bright cloud overshadowed them; and suddenly a voice came out of the

cloud, saying, "This is My beloved Son, in whom I am well pleased. Hear Him!" And when the disciples heard it, they fell on their faces and were greatly afraid. But Jesus came and touched them and said, "Arise, and do not be afraid." When they had lifted up their eyes, they saw no one but Jesus only. Now as they came from the mountain, Jesus commanded them, saying, "Tell the vision to no one until the Son of Man is risen from the dead." (The Son of Man is Jesus himself.)

Again, I highly encourage *all* readers of this book to study the Bible for yourself because I'm only capturing snapshots of the full story.

Luke 24:44–53 says,

> Then He said to them, "These are the words which I spoke to you while I was still with you, that all things must be fulfilled which were written in the Law of Moses and the Prophets and the Psalms concerning Me. And He opened their understanding, that they might comprehend the Scriptures. Then He said to them, "Thus it is written, and thus it was necessary for the Christ to suffer and to rise from the dead the third day, and that repentance and remission of sins should be preached in His name to all nations beginning at Jerusalem. And you are witnesses of these things. Behold, I send the Promise of My Father upon you; but tarry in the city of Jerusalem until you are endued with power from on high." And He led them out as far as Bethany, and He lifted up His hands and blessed them. Now it came to pass, while He blessed them, that He was parted from them and carried up heaven. And they worshiped Him and returned to Jerusalem with great

joy and were continually in the temple praising and blessing God. Amen.

The main point that I would like for you to see here in this passage from the Bible is verse 51: "Now it came to pass, while He (Jesus) blessed them, He (Jesus) was parted from them and carried up into heaven. The point being those that are there saw Him (Jesus) Ascend into Heaven."

Let's continue to explore the Scriptures referencing the testimonies and witnesses about Jesus being God.

Acts 1:21–22 says,

> "Therefore, of these men who have accompanied us all the time that the Lord Jesus went in and out among us, beginning from the baptism of John to that day when He was taken up from us, one of these must become a witness with us of His resurrection." And they proposed two: Joseph called Barsabas, who was surnamed Justus, and Matthias.

These two passages of scripture refer to the loss of Judas Iscariot because of his betrayal of Jesus for thirty pieces of silver and him later taking his own life and of the remaining eleven disciples of Jesus choosing one of the two men to take his place. The point being, the man that is to be chosen was with Jesus throughout His ministry, starting from the beginning, Jesus's baptism by John the Baptist, until His ascension into heaven.

Acts 13:30–31 says,

> But God raised Him from the dead. He was seen for many days by those who came up with Him from Galilee to Jerusalem, who are His witnesses to the people.

# CHAPTER 4

## My Misconceptions about Jesus before I Learned about the True Jesus of the Bible and the Trinity

Now would be a good time for me to explain who God really is. God is God the Father, God the Son (Jesus), and God the Holy Spirit (or the Holy Ghost) (KJV)—one God in three Persons. Now I understand that this concept might be a little hard for an average person to get their head wrapped around it. It was hard for me as well to understand, until I learned better by researching more. I started attending a Bible-centered church, which is more like a Bible school than a church; I started viewing more ministry shows on TV; and I started reading more of the Bible—all to aid me in focusing on what I learned previously in the Bible. I would highlight the Word of God with a bright yellow highlighter so the Words of Jesus would seem like they would jump off the page. Try it. You'll see what I mean.

Okay, before I dive back into the scriptures on the subject of Jesus being God, let's take a look at the wrong way that I would try to explain the three-person nature of God. For example, you the reader have parents, that would make you the son or daughter of your parents. If you are a worker, that would make you an employee of the company. If you have brothers or sisters, that would make you a sibling. If you have friends, that would make you a friend. What's my point? In all of these examples, it's still just you. You are the son or daughter of your parents; you are the worker at your place of employment; you are the brother or sister of your siblings; you are the friend to your friends—with you being the person wearing all these different hats so to speak. Again, the point is, in every example, the person was you. This way of thinking is completely wrong in relation to understanding the concept of one God in three Persons. That was my old way of attempting to explain how the multiple God of all creation could be just one. Again, I was very wrong in this way of thinking. This thought process is called modalism. Here's the definition modalism: (noun) the theological doctrine that the members of the Trinity are not three distinct persons but rather three modes or forms of activity (the Father, Son, and Holy Spirit) under which God manifest himself.

Another example of this way of thinking is a superhero character who is this mild-mannered person until danger strikes and then they change into their superhero uniform and become a crime fighter.

But this is not so with God. God is one God in three distinct Persons. He is omniscient, an all-knowing God. He is omnipotent, God possessing unlimited power able to do anything. He is omnipresent, God being present everywhere at once.

Later in this book, I'll show scripture references for God the Father; God the Son, who is Jesus; and God the Holy Spirit, or also called the Holy Ghost.

This one God, the God of *all creation*, is called the *Trinity*.

Before we explore more about *the real tri-union* God of *all creation, the Great I Am*, let me explain why the *Trinity* is so important. Because whatever your view is on the subject of the *Trinity*, it communicates your understanding of the basic Christian doctrines or if you agree with Christianity. The meaning of Christianity is the belief in Jesus Christ as the Son of God and Savior of the world and all of humanity of every nation, creed, and color.

Why does humanity need a Savior? Christianity teaches that there is only one God, and in the beginning, this God spoke the entire existence into being (Genesis chapters 1 and 2). Please read to get the full understanding. Here's an overview: God creates the first two people: a man named Adam and a woman named Eve. Their duties were to tend the Garden of Eden in which they lived. They were free to eat from any tree of the Garden except the tree of the knowable of good and evil (Genesis 2:15–17). In Genesis 3, sometime later, Satan tempts Eve to disobey God by lying to Eve and gets her to eat the fruit from the tree that God commanded them not to eat from. Then she gives some to her husband, Adam, and he eats it as well. It's at this point that the two become aware and now understand good and evil, evidenced by a new shame of their nakedness.

Disobeying God results in them being banished from the Garden and suffering the effects of spiritual death. Many generations later after Adam, God chooses a man named Abraham (Genesis 12) to make into a great nation. A nation that will one day birth a Messiah, a Savior to release mankind from the bondage of sin and death by believing on the name of Jesus Christ, the Messiah, the God of heaven and earth.

Isaiah 9:6–7 says,

> For unto us Child is born. Unto us a Son is given; and the government will be upon His shoulder. And His name will be called Wonderful, Counselor, Mighty God, Everlasting Father, Prince of Peace. Of the increase of His government and peace. There will be no end. Upon the throne of David and over His kingdom, to order it and establish it with judgment and justice from that time forward, even forever. The zeal of the Lord of Host will perform this.

But hold on, I'm getting ahead of myself. Let me continue to explain. Our modern-day calendar splits time at the approximate time of Jesus's birth. The term BC means before Christ, and AD means after death, or after Jesus's death.

Matthew 1:18–25 says,

> Now the birth of Jesus Christ was as follows: After His mother Mary was betrothed to Joseph, before they came together, she was found with

child of the Holy Spirit. Then Joseph her husband, being just man, and not wanting to make her a public example, was minded to put her away secretly. But while he thought about these things, behold, an angel of the Lord appeared to him in a dream, saying, "Joseph, son of David, do not be afraid to take to you Mary your wife, for that which is conceived in her is of the Holy Spirit. And she will bring forth a Son, and you shall call His name Jesus, for He will save His people from their sins. So all this was done that it might be fulfilled which was spoken by the Lord through the prophet, saying: 'Behold, the virgin shall be with child, and bear a Son, and they shall call His name Immanuel,' which is translated, 'God with us.'" Then Joseph, being aroused from sleep, did as the angel of the Lord commanded him and took to him his wife, and did not know her till she had brought forth her firstborn Son. And he called His name Jesus.

Christians believe in the coming Messiah. According to the New Testament of the Bible, Jesus is born to a virgin named Mary, lives a single life, and then willingly sacrifices Himself as the substitute, or an atonement, for all the sins of *all* mankind. The word *atonement* is used to describe an act that pays for or erases one's sins. The resurrected Christ appears to many people over the span of forty days before He bodily ascends to heaven from earth. He rules and reigns with God the Father and sends God the Holy Spirit to teach His followers. It is also maintained that one day Jesus will return to earth to judge *all* humans, living and dead, and grant eternal life to those who put their faith in Him alone.

Reference scripture:

> Jesus said to him, "I am the way the truth, and the life. No one comes to the Father except

> through Me. And eternal death in those who don't." (John 14:6)

> For God did not send His Son into the world to condemn the world, but that the world through Him might be saved. He who believes in Him is not condemned; but he who does not believe is condemned already, because he has not believed in the name of the only begotten Son of God. (John 3:17–18)

Christians call the message of Jesus Christ the Gospel, which means the Good News, and that is Christianity.

Now let me explain what the Trinity is. The Trinity is God the Father; God the Son, who is Jesus Christ, the Messiah; and God the Holy Spirit—one God in three Persons.

Reference scripture:

> Then God said, "Let Us make man in Our image, according to Our likeness; let them have dominion over the fish of the sea, over the birds of the air, and over the cattle, over all the earth and over every creeping thing that creeps on the earth." So God created man in His own image; in the image of God He created him male and female. He created them. (Genesis 1:26–27)

*Other scripture references:*

> But the Helper, the Holy Spirit, whom the Father will send in My name, He will teach you all things, and bring to your remembrance all things that I said to you. (John 14:26)

> But when the Helper comes, whom I shall send to you from the Father, the Spirit of truth

> who proceeds from the Father, he will testify of Me. (John 15:26)

> The grace of the Lord Jesus Christ, and the love of God, and the communion of the Holy Spirit be with you all. Amen. (2 Corinthians 13:14)

> For there are three that bear witness in heaven: the Father, the Word, and the Holy Spirit; and these three are one. (1 John 5:7)

There are other passages I could use as well. The last one I will use to illustrate the fact of the Trinity God being one God in three Persons:

> Go therefore and make disciples of all the nations, baptizing them in the name of the Father and the of the Son and of the Holy Spirit. (Matthew 28:19)

This is very important to understand, because if you or someone that your listening to rejects the truth of the Trinity, it not a minor issue. You have to ask now yourself what other major aspects, beliefs, or tenets of the Christian faith that this person also believe or subscribe to, which is going to lead you to the question of whether or not you should be putting yourself under that person's teaching.

Here are four simple and clear statements that you must adhere to, if you are going to subscribe to the biblical belief of the Trinity.

Number one, there is only true God. The definition of the Trinity is GOD is *One* in *Being* and in three in *Person*. Deuteronomy 6:4–5 says, "Hear, O Israel: The Lord our God, the Lord is one! You shall love the Lord your God with all your heart, with all your soul, and with all your strength." This passage of scripture is called the Shema, which every Hebrew was taught to recite both in the morning and in the evening. So to deny that there is only one God makes you a polytheist. Here's the definition of *polytheist*: (noun) belief in or worship of more than one god. The true God hates this because He is a jealous God. Scripture reference is Exodus 34:14, "For you shall worship no other god, for the Lord, whose name is Jealous, is a jealous God." Please notice when you read the Bible, you'll see that the one True God's name all start with capital letters, whether it's God the Father or God the Son, Jesus, or God the Holy Spirit. I just thought that I would point that out.

Now let's continue. Judaism is a monotheistic religion. Here's the definition of *monotheistic*: (adjective) relating to or characterized by the belief that there is only one God. Christianity was birthed out of the Jewish faith or belief. Christianity also subscribes to the fact that there is only one True God. Thus, the title of my book is *Jesus Is God*. This fact is actually where many other religions differ from the true gospel of Jesus Christ, which is the Christian faith or belief. I'll note here also Christianity is not a religion, but a daily walk with the Living God, Jesus Christ. Scripture reference is Colossians 2:6–7, "As you therefore have received Christ Jesus the Lord, so walk in Him, rooted and built up in Him and established in the faith, as you have been taught, abounding in it with thanksgiving."

Now onto examples of how other so-called religions differ from what's real. For example, the Mormons believe that any human being can ascend to become a god and can become a god of a different planet and give birth to other children and those children can become gods as well. This information can be found in the Mormon writing *The Teaching of Joseph Smith* (345–354) and *Doctrines and Convents* (132:20). This is a *false* teaching, and the Mormons do not follow the true Gospel of Jesus Christ found in the Holy Bible. Any person (or group) that teaches anything other than the true doctrine of Jesus Christ is a false teacher and a liar. There is a warning in the Bible that speaks to this fact. Galatians 1:3–9 says,

> Grace to you and peace from God the Father and our Lord Jesus Christ, who gave Himself for our sins, that He might deliver us from this present evil age, according to the will of our God and

> Father, to whom be glory forever and ever. Amen. I marvel that you are turning away so soon from Him who called you in the grace of Christ, to a different gospel, which is not another; but there are some who trouble you and want to pervert the gospel of Christ. But even if we, or an angel from heaven, preach any other gospel to you than what we have preached to you, let him be accursed. As we have said before, so now I say again, if anyone preaches any other gospel to you than what you have received, let him be accursed.

The second statement that you might adhere to is that there is one God who coexist eternally in three Persons. Here's a scripture reference:

> When all the people were baptized, it came to pass that Jesus also was baptized; and while He prayed, the heaven was opened, And the Holy Spirit descended in bodily form like a dove upon Him, and voice came from heaven which said, "You are My beloved Son; in You I am well pleased. (Luke 3:21–22)

As you can see in this passage, it speaks of God the Son (Jesus); God the Father, who spoke from heaven; and God the Holy Spirit.

Let's continue. Now the key word in the statement is *eternally*, which means there was never a time in eternity past or there will never be a time in eternity future where God the Father, God the Son (Jesus), or God the Holy Spirit did not exist. Here's a Scripture reference from Genesis. *Genesis* means the beginning, so back in the beginning of the Bible. Genesis chapter 11:7 says, "Come, let Us go down and there confuse their language, that they may not understand one another's speech." This is yet another place where other religions differ from Orthodox Christianity. For example, Jehovah's Witness, the Mormons, and others believe that Jesus did not exist eternally; but rather, they believe Jesus was a created being. This is flat-out not true. Here are four verses as scripture reference:

> For unto us a Child is born, Unto us a Son is given; And the government will be upon His shoulders. And His name will be called Wonderful, Counselor, Mighty God, Everlasting Father, Prince of Peace. (Isaiah 9:6)

And in the book of Revelation, which is located at the very end of the Bible, are three verses:

> And behold, I am coming quickly, and My reward is with Me, to give to every one according to his work. I am the Alpha and the Omega. The Beginning and the End, the First and the Last. (Revelation 22:12–13)

> I Jesus, have sent My angel to testify to you these things in the churches. I am the root and the Offspring of David the Bright and Morning Star. (Revelation 22:16)

The other false religions' beliefs are a direct violation and are a contradiction to the Word of God, which describes Jesus clearly as the uncreated Creator. Here are three reference scriptures:

> Jesus said to them, "Most assuredly, I say to you, before Abraham was I Am." (John 8:58)

> And now, O Father, glorify Me together with Yourself, with the glory which I had with You before the world was. (John 17:5)

> Father, I desire that they also whom You gave Me may be with Me where I am, that they

*may behold My glory which You have given Me; for You loved Me before the foundation of the world.* (John 17:24)

The third statement that you must believe is that there is one God who coexists eternally in three distinct Persons. This just simply means that God the Father is different or distinct or separate from God the Son (Jesus), who is different or distinct or separate from God the Holy Spirit, who is different from God the Father. All of them are different Persons or members of the Godhead that is God.

First John 5:7 says, "For there are three that bear witness in heaven: the Father, the Word, and the Holy Spirit; and these three are one." In this scripture passage, it speaks of the God the Father; God the Son, as the Word of God; and God the Holy Spirit.

Let me take a little time to back up that the Word of God is in fact Jesus. John 1:1–3 says, "In the beginning was the Word, and the Word was with God, and the Word was God. He was in the beginning with God. All things were made through Him, and without Him nothing was made that was made." Now if we skip down to verse 14, it says, "And the Word became flesh and dwelt among us, and we beheld His glory, the as of the only begotten of the Father, full of grace and truth." This is also the reason why no one should refer to the Holy Spirit as an it or a something because He is just as much Person and a member of the Trinity as God the Father and God the Son (Jesus).

The Bible says that God the Holy Spirit can speak to us. For example, Luke 12:12 says, *"For the Holy Spirit will teach you in that very hour what you ought to say."* The Bible also says that God the Holy Spirit is one that can be grieved. Ephesians 4:29–30 says, "Let no corrupt word proceed out of your mouth, but what is good for necessary edification, that it may impart grace to the hearers. And do not grieve the Holy Spirit of God, by whom you were sealed for the day of redemption." Again, the Holy Spirit is not just some force, and He is not just some it. He is actually a Person of the Trinity. Mark 13:11 says, *"But when they arrest you and deliver you up, do not worry beforehand, or premeditate what you will speak. But whatever* is given you in that hour, speak that; for it is not you who speak, but the Holy Spirit."

Now I would like to also focus in on another word in this statement, which is the word *coexists*. This means that God the Father, and God the Son (Jesus), and God the Holy Spirit are *all* existing, or coexisting, at the same time. First Peter 1:2 says, "Elect according to the foreknowledge of God the Father, in sanctification of the Spirit, for obedience and sprinkling of the blood of Jesus Christ: Grace to you and peace be multiplied." Many centuries ago, people tried to best understand the Trinity and came up with false teaching called modalism. Again, this is the idea that God can only exist in one mode at one time, like the analogy I shared earlier about the superhero changing into their costume. It's the idea that God changes His identity from one to the other. I must admit I use to think this way but not anymore. The scripture references I shared previously shows this is a wrong way of thinking. For the people that believe this, I just want you to know that this is a false teaching and a wrong understanding of the Trinity. The truth of God are clearly shown in the scriptures I shared. Open up the Bible and see for yourself. Never believe the words of anyone about Jesus unless they can prove it to you in the Bible. Being a Christian is a lifelong commitment, and studying and reading the Bible is vital for proper spiritual growth and a proper relationship with God.

The fourth and final statement you need to understand about the Trinity is that there is one God that coexists eternally in three distinct Persons who are coequal. This just simply means that God the Father, God the Son (Jesus), and God the Holy Spirit are all equal in there essence, or in the their deity, is another way to say it. They have different roles, but all One I Am. God the Father does not have the same role as God the Son (Jesus), and God the Son (Jesus) does not have the same role as God the Holy Spirit. A great picture of how it works is a great marriage. For example, the husband and the wife are equal in terms of their fidelity or union to one another. But they have different roles that have been assigned to each one to carry out the vision of the marriage. Let me be clear, God isn't a marriage. That was just an example of roles. If I had to try to describe God being three-in-one God. Today, I might say it this way: God the Father creates the plan, Jesus Christ implements the plan, and the Holy Spirit administers the plan.

# CHAPTER 5

## What Is the Meaning of the Trinity

Now that we have taken a look at the Trinity and now understand that the Trinity is the One True God revealed in three Persons of God the Father, God the Son (Jesus Christ, the Savior of the World), and God the Holy Spirit, in this chapter, I would like to reveal scriptures that will unveil more of God.

Deuteronomy 6:4–25 says,

> Hear, O Israel: The Lord our God, the Lord is one! You shall love the Lord your God with all your heart, with all your soul, and with all your strength. And these words which I command you today shall be in your heart. You shall teach them diligently to your children, and shall talk of them when you sit in your house, when you walk by the way, when you lie down, and when you rise up. You shall bind them as a sign on your hand, and they shall be as frontlets between your eyes. You shall write them on the doorposts of your house and on your gates. So it shall be, when the lord your God brings you into the land of which He swore to your fathers, to Abraham, Isaac, and Jacob, to give you large and beautiful cities which you did not build. Houses falloff all good things,

which you did not fill, hewn-out wells which you did not dig, vineyards and olive trees which you did not plant when you have eaten and are full then beware, lest you forget the Lord who brought you out of the land of Egypt, from the house of bondage. You shall fear the Lord your God and serve Him, and shall take oaths in his name. You shall not go after other gods, the gods of the peoples who are all around you (for the Lord your God is a jealous God among you), lest the anger of the Lord your God be aroused against you and destroy you from the face of the earth. You shall not tempt the Lord your God as you tempted Him in Messiah. You shall diligently keep the commandments of the Lord your God, His testimonies, and His statutes which He has commanded you. And you shall do what is right and good in the sight of the Lord, that it may be well with you, and that you may go in and possess the good land of which the Lord swore to your fathers, to cast out all your enemies from before you, as the Lord has spoken. When your son asks you in time to come, saying, "What is the meaning of the testimonies, the statutes, and the judgments which the Lord our God has commanded you?" Then you shall say to your son: "We were slaves of Pharaoh in Egypt, and the Lord brought us out of Egypt with a mighty hand; and the Lord showed signs and wonders before our eyes, great and severe, against Egypt, Pharaoh, and all his household. Then He brought us out from there, that He might bring us in to give us the land of which He swore to our fathers. And the Lord commanded us to observe all these statutes, to fear the Lord our God, for our good always, that He might preserve us alive, as it is this day. Then it will be righteousness for us if we are careful to observe all these commandments before the Lord our God, as He has commanded us."

## Other Scripture References

*New Testament*

Let nothing be done through selfish ambition or conceit, but in lowliness of mind let each esteem others better than himself. Let each of you look out not only for his own interests, but also for the interests of others. Let this mind be in you which was also in Christ Jesus, who, being in the form of God, did not consider it robbery to be equal with God, but made Himself of no reputation, taking the form of a bondservant, and coming in the likeness of men. And being found in appearance as a man, He humbled Himself and became obedient to the point of death, even the death of the cross. Therefore, God also has highly exalted Him and given Him the name which is above every name, that at the name of Jesus every knee should bow, of those in heaven, and of those on earth, and of those under the earth, and that every tongue should confess that Jesus Christ is Lord, to the glory of God the Father. (Philippians 2:4–11)

*Old Testament*

Thus says the Lord, the King of Israel, and his Redeemer, the Lord of host; "I am the First and I'm the Last; besides Me there is no God." (Isaiah 44:6)

## JESUS IS GOD

Thus says the Lord, your Redeemer, and He who formed you from the womb: "I am the Lord, who makes all things, Who stretches out the heavens all alone, Who spreads abroad the earth by Myself." (Isaiah 44:24)

Look to Me, and be saved, all you ends of the earth! For I am God, and there is no other. I have sworn by Myself; the word has gone out of My mouth in righteousness, and shall not return, that to Me every knee shall bow, every tongue shall take an oath. (Isaiah 45:22–23)

*New Testament*

And the high priest stood up in the midst and asked Jesus, saying, "Do You answer nothing? What is it these men testify against You?" But He kept silent and answered nothing. Again the high priest asked Him, saying to Him, "Are You the Christ, the Son of the Blessed?" Jesus said, "I am And you will see the Son of Man sitting at the right hand of the Power, and coming with the clouds of heaven." (Mark 14:60–62)

*Old Testament*

I was watching in the night visions, and behold, One like the Son of Man, come with the clouds of heaven! He came to the Ancient of Days, and they brought Him near before Him. Then to Him was given dominion and glory and a kingdom, that all people, nation, and languages should serve Him. His dominion is an everlasting dominion, which shall not pass away, and His kingdom the one which shall not be destroyed. (Daniel 7:13–14)

# CHAPTER 6

## CHRISTIANS: WHO ARE THEY AND WHAT DO CHRISTIANS HAVE TO DO WITH JESUS?

Like previously mentioned, Judaism is a monotheistic religion, and Christianity was birthed out of the Jewish faith, which also believes that there is only one God. A dictionary definition of a Christian would be something similar to a person professing a belief in Jesus as the Christ or the Messiah or the Anointed One.

The word *Christian* is in the New Testament three times:

> Then Barnabas departed for Tarsus to seek Saul. And when he had found him, he brought him to Antioch. So it was that for a whole year they assembled with the church and taught a great many people. And the disciples were first called Christians in Antioch. (Acts 11:25–26)

> Then Agrippa said to Paul, "You almost persuade me to become a Christian." (Acts 26:28)

> Yet if anyone suffers as a Christian, let him not be ashamed, but let him glorify God in this matter. (1 Peter 4:16)

The word *Christian* literally means belonging to the party of Christ or a follower of Christ.

1) A Christian should be someone that believes in God the Father, God the Son (Jesus Christ), and God the Holy Spirit.
2) A Christian should profess their faith in the biblical Jesus of the Bible.
3) A Christian should follow Jesus and live a holy life every day. Luke 9:23–27 says, "Then He said to them all, 'If anyone desires to come after Me, let him deny himself, and take up his cross daily, and follow Me.' For whoever desires to save his life will lose it, but whoever loses his life for My sake will save it. For what profits is it to a man if he gains the whole world, and is himself destroyed or lost? For whoever is ashamed of Me and My words, of him the Son of Man will be ashamed when He comes in His own glory, and in His Father's and of the holy angels. But I tell you truly, there are some standing here who shall not taste death till they see the kingdom of God."
4) Being a Christian is a lifestyle, having a relationship with God, by reading His Word, the Holy Bible, and following the teaching of Jesus Christ.
5) Being a Christian is your true identity. It's your status. It's who you are as a person of the Christian faith.

Christianity is all about Jesus Christ, and everything else is rooted in that fact. The Bible is a book about Christ (Jesus). The rules of Christianity are about being like Jesus, or Christlike.

## The Practices of Christianity

*Holy Communion*

> For I received from the Lord that which I also delivered to you: that the Lord Jesus on

the same night in which He was betrayed took bread; and when He had given thanks, He broke it and said, "Take, eat; this is My body which is broken for you; do this in remembrance of Me." In the same manner He also took the cup after supper, saying, "This cup is the new covenant in My blood. This do, as often as you drink it, in remembrance of Me." For as often as you eat this bread and drink this cup, you proclaim the Lord's death till He comes. Therefore whoever eats this bread or drinks this cup of the Lord in an unworthy manner will be guilty of the body and blood of the Lord. But let a man examine himself, and so let him eat of the bread and drink of the cup. For he who eats and drinks in an unworthy manner eats and drinks judgement to himself, not discerning the Lord's body. For this reason many are weak and sick among you, and many sleep. For if we would judge ourselves, we would not be judged. But when we are judged, we are chastened by the Lord, that we may not be condemned with the world. (1 Corinthians 11:23–32)

*Baptism*

Therefore, we were buried with Him through baptism into death, that just as Christ was raised from the dead by the glory of the Father, even so we also should walk in newness of life. (Romans 6:4)

For in Him dwells all the fullness of the Godhead bodily; and you are complete in Him, who is the head of all principality and power. In Him you were also circumcised with the circumcision made without hands, by putting off the body of the sins of the flesh, by the circumcision of Christ, buried with Him in baptism, in which you also were raised with Him through faith in the working of God, who raised Him from the dead. And you, being dead in your trespasses and the uncircumcision of your flesh, He has made alive together with Him, having forgiven you all trespasses. (Colossians 2:9–13)

He who believes and is baptized will be saved; but he who does not believe will be condemned. (Mark 16:16)

Jesus was baptized by John the Baptist.

Then Jesus came from Galilee to John at the Jordan to be baptized by him. And John tried to prevent Him, saying, "I need to be baptized by You, and are You coming to me?" But Jesus answered and said to him, "Permit it to be so now, for thus it is fitting for us to fulfill all righteousness," then he allowed Him. (Matthew 3:13–17)

Communion and baptism are about being united with Jesus. The church is the kingdom of Christ Jesus here on earth, and heaven is a participation in the eternal life of Jesus that He achieved by rising from the dead. So if Christianity is all about Jesus (John 14:6 says, "Jesus said to him, 'I am the way, the truth, and the life. No one comes to the Father except through Me.'"), then who is He? As previously mentioned in chapter 1, Jesus is the Son of God. John 10:30 says, "I and My Father are One," which makes Him truly God.

And He was also born to a human mother. Luke1:30–38 says,

> Then the angel said to her, "Do not be afraid, Mary, for you have found favor with God. "And behold, you will conceive in your womb and bring forth a Son, and shall call His name Jesus. "He will be great, and will be called the Son of the Highest; and the Lord God will give Him the throne of His father David. "And He will reign over the house of Jacob forever, and of His kingdom there will be no end." Then Mary said to the angel, "How can this be, since I do not know a man?" And the angel answered and said to her, "The Holy Spirit will come upon you, and the power of the Highest will overshadow you; therefore, also that Holy One who is to be born will be called the Son of God. Now indeed, Elizabeth your relative has also conceived a son in her old age; and this is now the sixth mouth for her who was called barren. For with God nothing will be impossible." Then Mary said, "Behold the maidservant of the Lord! Let it be to me according to your word." And the angel departed from her.

This makes Him truly human, a human just like the rest of us. Because He is truly human and truly God, He is the only One that can bridge the gap between God and humanity. One might say, "Well, if He is the Son of God, then how is He also God?" Because as was previously stated, God is Father, Son, and Holy Spirit—one Being or Godhead, one God in three Persons. This is called the Trinity (Tri-Unity). This explains how Jesus can be God and also worship God. He worshiped God here on earth because humans are created to worship God.

> This people I have formed for Myself; they shall declare My praise. He was the only perfect Human Man without sin. Jesus healed the sick. (Isaiah 43:21)

> But when Jesus knew it, He withdrew from there. And great multitude followed Him, and He healed them all. Jesus casted out demons. (Matthew 12:15)

> And He was casting out a demon, and it was mute. So it was, when the demon had gone out, that the mute spoke; and the multitudes marveled. Jesus opened the eyes of the blind. And that very hour He cured many of infirmities, afflictions, and evil spirits; and to many blind He gave sight. (Luke 11:14)

Eventually, people realized that He was the Messiah, or also known as the Christ that the prophets predicted would come. Matthew 1:1–15 speaks of the fourteen generations until the birth of Christ Jesus. Isaiah 9:6 says, "For unto us a Child is born, Unto us a Son is given; And the government will be upon His shoulder. And His name will be called Wonderful, Counselor, Mighty God, Everlasting Father, Prince of Peace."

Jesus ministered the kingdom of God. Matthew 6:30 33 says,

> Now if God so clothes the grass of the field, which today is, and tomorrow is thrown into the oven, will He not much more clothe you, O you of little faith? Therefore do not worry, saying, "What shall we eat?" Or "What shall we drink?" Or "What shall we wear?" For after all

> these things the Gentiles seek. For your heavenly Father knows that you need all these things. But seek first the kingdom of God and His righteousness, and all these things shall be added to you. Therefore do not worry about tomorrow, for tomorrow will worry about its own things. Sufficient for the day is its own trouble.

The religious leader of that time didn't like Jesus challenging their authority, and they wanted to kill Him on a cross. Now Jesus could have stopped this at any time, but He didn't. Matthew 26:52–54 says,

> But Jesus said to him, "Put your sword in its place, for all who take the sword will perish by the sword. Or do you think that I cannot now pray to My Father, and He will provide Me with more than twelve legions of angels? How then could the Scriptures be fulfilled, that it must happen thus?

This part of scripture here describes Jesus and the disciples in the Garden of Gethsemane just before He was taken by the soldiers. Jesus informs Peter that He has the ability to pray to God the Father in heaven to send twelve legions of angels to help Him. But He said it needed to happen. Why did Jesus have to die? Because the world and everything God created is filled with evil or sin from the original sin of Adam and Eve. To gain better understanding of this, please read Genesis chapter 2, the whole chapter. Because of what took place with Adam and Eve, the first two humans created by God, every other person that was born after them took on the nature of sin as well. However, the Good News—or even better word to use is, the Gospel of Jesus Christ—is that Jesus died as a sacrifice to pay the price for all of our sins so that all our debts of sin can be forgiven. Because it has been paid for in full by Jesus's death on the cross, burial, and resurrection, we can live in a redeemed creation forever, if whosoever accepts Jesus Christ as their Lord and Savior.

Again, why did Jesus die? To sacrifice Himself for all people—every creed, every color from all nations of the world. He even died for the people who hated Him, that put Him on the cross to be crucified. Whosoever that will believe on His name (Jesus) choose Him as their Lord and Savior. On the third day, Jesus rose from the dead, triumphing over sin, evil, and the grave. Colossians 2:15 says,

> Having disarmed principalities and powers, He made a public spectacles of them, triumphing over them in it. Making redemption, and eternal life possible for All human kind which chooses Jesus as there Lord and Savior.

Jesus holds the whole world together. Colossians 1:17–20 says,

> And He is before all things, and in Him all things consist. And He is the head of the body, the church, who is the beginning, the firstborn from the dead, that in all things He may have the preeminence. For it pleased the Father that in Him all the fulness should dwell, and by Him to reconcile all things to Himself, by Him, whether things on earth or things in heaven, having made peace through the blood of His cross.

## The Resurrection of Jesus

> Because the creation itself also will be delivered from the bondage of corruption into the glorious liberty of the children of God. Jesus resurrection brings with it the resurrection of the entire world. That means anyone that has chosen Jesus to be their Lord and Savior or have placed their faith in Christ will also be raised from the

dead, and also will have eternal life. (Romans 8:21)

> Therefore we were buried with Him through baptism into death, that just as Christ was raised from the dead by the glory of the Father, even so we also should walk in newness of life. For if we have been united together in the likeness of His death, certainly we also shall be in the likeness of His resurrection, knowing this, that our old man was crucified with Him, that the body of sin might be done away with, that we should no longer be slaves of sin. For he who has died has been freed from sin. Now if we died with Christ, we believe that we shall also live with Him, knowing that Christ, having been raised from the dead, dies no more. Death no longer has dominion over Him. For the death that He died, He died to sin once for all; but the life that He lives, He lives to God. Likewise you also, reckon yourselves to be dead indeed to sin, but alive to God in Christ Jesus our Lord. (Romans 6:4–11)

Forty days after Jesus's resurrection, Jesus ascended back into heaven. Why did He do that? To be seated at the right hand of the Father, to rule over His kingdom, while the God the Holy Spirit is here on earth, leading, guiding, and bringing to the remembrance all the teachings of Jesus to the people here on earth. John 14:26 says,

> But the Helper, the Holy Spirit, whom the Father will send in My name, He will teach you all things, and bring to your remembrance all things that I said to you. Because He wants to involve His people in the work of spreading the kingdom, or the Gospel, the Good news in redeeming the world.

# JESUS IS GOD

In anticipation of Jesus's return to the earth, how can people spread the kingdom? At Pentecost, Jesus sent God the Holy Spirit to His people here on earth to empower them to build the church, which is the kingdom of God here on earth. So anyone that has faith in Jesus Christ, God the Holy Spirit unites them to Jesus Christ, through Bible teaching, leading, and guiding. Romans 8:14 says, "For as many as are led by the Spirit of God, these are sons of God." John 16:13–15 says,

> However, when He, the Spirit of truth, has come, He will guide you into all truth; for He will not speak on His own authority, but whatever He hears He will speak; and He will tell you things to come. He will glorify Me, for He will take of what is Mine and declare it to you. All things that the Father has are Mine. Therefore, I said that He will take of Mine and declare it to you.

Being a Christian means being citizen of God's kingdom; and this involves helping the poor; resisting evil; and spreading the Gospel (the teaching of Jesus), which is sharing the Good News. And true Christians followers of Jesus Christ do this in the hope that *all* evil will be destroyed and *all* good things will be fully restored before the fall of mankind, when sin came into the world.

So if you want to become a Christian, you have to believe the Good News. Here it is broken down for you in seven steps.

- Step 1: You have to be willing to repent of all your sins. Luke 13:3 says, "I tell you, no; but unless you repent you will all likewise perish."
- Step 2: Believe that Jesus came to this earth from heaven, born of a virgin mother. Matthew 1:18 says, "Now the birth of Jesus Christ was as follows: After His mother Mary was betrothed to Joseph, before they came together, she was found with child of the Holy Spirit."

Step 3: To gain better understanding of God and His Word, please read the Bible. If I was just starting, I would start with Matthew, Mark, Luke, and John. These four books of the Bible are called the Gospels. Joshua 1:8 says, "This Book of the Law shall not depart from your mouth, but you shall meditate in it day and night, that you may observe to do according to all that is written in it For then you will make your way prosperous, and then you will have good success."

Step 4: You should attend an awesome Bible-believing church who not afraid to speak to the truth in love to the people regardless to what's trending in society that may water down the words of Jesus. Psalm 27:4 says, "One thing I have desired of the Lord, that will I seek: That May dwell in the house of the Lord All the days of my life, To behold the beauty of the Lord, And to inquire in His temple."

Step 5: Participate in GOD's kingdom—or another way to say it could be God's way of doing life—based on the teachings of His Word. John 14:15 says, "If you love Me, keep my commandments," and 1 Peter 3:21–22 says, "There is also an antitype which now saves us baptism not the removal of the filth of the flesh, but the answer of a good conscience toward God), through the resurrection of Jesus Christ. who has gone into heaven and is at the right hand of God, angels and authorities and powers having been made subject to Him."

Step 6: You should get water baptized. This is public showing to all people that you belong to Jesus. Water baptism also represents that Jesus hung on a cross, died, and was buried for our sins. It's a representation for new believers that when Jesus was buried and the new believer goes down into the water (the old person), they come up new in Christ Jesus. Matthew 3:13 and 17 says, "Then Jesus came from Galilee to John at the Jorden to be baptized by him," and "And suddenly a voice came from heaven saying, 'This is My beloved Son in whom I'm well pleased.'"

Step 7: The Bible says that to covet the best gifts and those awesome gifts from God entails praying in God's heavenly language, or better known as praying in the Holy Spirit. First Corinthians 12:31 says, "But earnestly desire the best gifts. And yet Show you a more excellent way," and Jude 20–21 says, "But you, beloved, building yourselves up on your most holy faith, praying in the Holy Spirit, keep yourselves in the love of God, looking for the mercy of our Lord Jesus Christ unto eternal life."

Now nobody ever said it would be easy. You might even suffer persecution. Taking this stand for Christ, however, for so many people means finding everlasting hope in Jesus Christ, which is greater than all the things that this world has to offer. Eternal life with your Creator in heaven is your reward for anyone who would like to become a Christian.

Let's pray the prayer of salvation. Believe it in your heart and say with your mouth, for Romans 10:9–10 says, "That if you confess with your mouth the Lord Jesus and believe in your heart that God has raised Him from the dead, you will be saved. For with the heart one believes unto righteousness, and with the mouth confession is made unto salvation," and Romans 10:13 says, "For whoever calls on the name of the Lord shall be saved."

Let's pray.

> Dear Heavenly Father, in the name of Jesus, I do believe that Jesus Christ is the Son of God and that He came to earth from heaven for the remission of sins for all the people of the world and that He died and was buried and rose on the third day, paying the full price for sin, for whosoever would believe in Jesus Christ Savior of the whole world.
>
> Lord Jesus, come into my heart and save me now. I repent of all sin. I apologize, Lord, and I'm willing to accept your offer of forgiveness. Thank

you, Lord, for saving me, and forgiving me. I am willing to live for you from this day forward in Jesus's name, Amen, Amen, Amen. One for God the Father, one for God the Son (Jesus), and one for God the Holy Spirit.

Congratulations! Welcome to the family of God! To continue to grow in your faith with Jesus Christ, I would strongly suggest that you join a good Bible-believing church that is not afraid to teach you the uncompromising word of God from the Bible because the Bible is God speaking to His people. Read the Holy Bible every day. Pray to the Father, in the name of Jesus, on what to read for that day. May God bless you *all* in the name of Jesus.

# CHAPTER 7

## SCRIPTURES ON GOD THE FATHER

In the next three chapters, starting with this chapter, I'm going to show scripture references that feature God the Father, God the Son (Jesus), and God the Holy Spirit, in an effort to color in the picture of God more vividly and to hopefully in encourage the reading of God's Word, the Holy Bible, daily. (Some of the scripture references may have been previously mention in other parts of this book.)

Now let's take a look at scriptures that feature God the Father.

> For God so loved the world that He gave His only begotten Son, the whoever believes in Him should not perish but have everlasting life. For God did not send His Son into the world to condemn the world, but that the world through Him might be saved. (John 3:16–17)

> Do not call anyone on earth your father; for One is your Father, He who is in heaven. (Matthew 23:9)

> A Father of the fatherless, a defender of widows, is God in His holy habitation. (Psalm 68:5)

But now, O Lord, You are our Father; We are the clay, and You our potter; and all we are the work of Your hand. (Isaiah 64:8)

Blessed be the God and Father of our Lord Jesus Christ, who has blessed us with every spiritual blessing in the heavenly places in Christ. (Ephesians 1:3)

Every good gift and every perfect gift is from above, and comes down from the Father of lights, with whom there is no variation or shadow of turning. (James 1:17)

Doubtless You are our Father, though Abraham was ignorant of us, and Israel does not acknowledge us. You, O Lord, are our Father; Our Redeemer from Everlasting is Your name. (Isaiah 63:16)

Blessed be the God and Father of our Lord Jesus Christ, who according to His abundant mercy has begotten us again to a living hope through the resurrection of Jesus Christ from the dead. (1 Peter 1:3)

Behold what manner of love the Father has bestowed on us, that we should be called children of God! Therefore, the world does not know us, because it did not know Him. (1 John 3:1)

In that hour Jesus rejoiced in the Spirit and said, "I thank You, Father, Lord of heaven and earth, that You have hidden these things from the wise and prudent and revealed them to babes. Even so, Father, for so it seemed good in Your sight. All things have been delivered to Me by My Father, and no one knows who the Son is except the Father, and who the Father is except the Son, and the one to whom the Son wills to reveal him." (Luke 10:21–22)

I will be a Father to you, and you shall be My sons and daughters, says the Lord Almighty. (2 Corinthians 6:18)

In the beginning was the Word, and the Word was with God, and the Word was God. (John 1:1)

Jesus said to her, "Do not cling to Me, for I have not yet ascended to My Father; but go to My brethren and say to them, 'I am ascending to My Father and your Father, and to My God and your God.'" (John 20:17)

Thus says the Lord, the King of Israel, and his Redeemer, the Lord of hosts: "I am the First and I am the Last; besides Me there is no God." (Isaiah 44:6)

And He said, "Abba, Father, all things are possible for You. Take this cup away from Me; nevertheless, not what will, but what You will." (Mark 14:36)

Jesus answered and said to him, "If anyone loves Me, he will keep My word; and My Father will love him, and We will come to him and make Our home with him. He who does not love Me does not keep My words; and the word which you hear is not Mine but the Father who sent Me. (John 14:23–24)

Then a voice came from heaven, "You are My beloved Son, in whom I am well pleased." (Mark 1:11)

Do not fear, little flock, for it is your Father's good pleasure to give you the kingdom. (Luke 12:32)

If you then, being evil, know how to give good gifts to your children, how much more will your Father who is in heaven give good things to those who ask Him! (Matthew 7:11)

Are not two sparrows sold for a copper coin? And not one of them falls to the ground apart from your Father's will. But the very hairs of your head are all numbered. Do not fear therefore; you are of more value than many sparrows. Therefore whoever confesses Me before men, him I will also confess before My Father who is in heaven. (Matthew 10:29–32)

But you, when you pray, go into your room, and when you have shut your door, pray to your Father who is in the secret place; and your Father who sees in secret will reward you openly. (Matthew 6:6)

In this manner, therefore, pray: Our Father in heaven hallowed be Your name. Your kingdom come. Your will be done On earth as it is in heaven. Give us this day our daily bread. And forgive us our debts, As we forgive our debtors.

# JESUS IS GOD

*And do not lead us into temptation, but deliver us from the evil one. For Yours is the kingdom and the power and the glory forever. Amen. For if you forgive men their trespasses, your heavenly Father will also forgive you. But if you do not forgive men their trespasses, neither will your Father forgive your trespasses.* (Matthew 6:9–15)

That you may with one mind and one mouth glorify the God and Father of our Lord Jesus Christ. (Romans 15:6)

*He who has My commandments and keeps them, it is he who loves Me and he who loves Me will be loved by My Father, and I will love him and manifest Myself to him.* (Matthew 14:21)

"You do the deeds of your father." Then they said to Him, "Were not born of fornication; we have one Father-God." Jesus said to them, *"If God were your Father, you would love Me, for proceeded forth and came From God; nor have I come of Myself, but He sent Me."* (John 8:41–42)

*Heaven and earth will pass away, but My words will by no means pass away. But of that day and hour no one knows, not even the angels of heaven, but My Father only.* (Mathew 24:35–36)

*And whatever you ask in My name, that I will do, that the Father may be glorified in the Son.* (John 14:13)

# CHAPTER 8

## God the Son (Jesus): The Teachings of Jesus

And Thomas answered and said to Him, "My Lord and my God!" Jesus said to him, "Thomas, because you have seen Me, you have believed. Blessed are those who have not seen and yet have believed." (John 20:28–29)

Looking for the blessed hope and glorious appearing of our great God and Savior Jesus Christ. (Titus 2:13)

"I and My Father are one." Then the Jews took up stones again to stone Him. Jesus answered them, "Many good works I have shown you from My Father. For which of those works do you stone Me?" The Jews answered Him, saying, "For a good work we do not stone You but for blasphemy, and because You, being a Man, make Yourself God." Jesus answered them, "Is it not written in your law, 'I said, "You are gods"'? If He called them gods, to whom the word of God came (and the Scripture cannot be broken), do you say of Him whom the Father sanctified and sent into the world, 'You are blaspheming,'

## JESUS IS GOD

because I said, 'I am the Son of God'? If I do not do the works of My Father, do not believe Me; but if I do, though you do not believe Me, believe the works, that you may know and believe that the Father is in Me, and I in Him." (John 10:30–38)

Who being the brightness of His glory and the express image of His person, and upholding all things by the word of His power, when He had by Himself purged our sins, sat down at the right hand of the Majesty on high. (Hebrews 1:3)

In the beginning was the Word, and the Word was with God, and the Word was God. (John 1:1)

And the Word became flesh and dwelt among us, and we beheld His glory, the glory as of the only begotten of the Father, full of grace and truth. (John 1:14)

In My Father's house are many mansions; if it were not so, I would have told you. I go to prepare a place for you. And if I go and prepare a place for you, I will come again and receive you to Myself; that where I am, there you may be also. (John 14:2–3)

Jesus said to him, "I am the way, the truth, and the life. No one comes to the Father except through Me." (John 14:6)

He said to them, "But who do you say that I am?" Simon Peter answered and said, "You are the Christ, the Son of the living God." Jesus answered and said to him, "Blessed are you,

Simon Bar-Jonah, for flesh and blood has not revealed this to you, but My Father who is in heaven." (Matthew 16:15–17)

And without controversy great is the mystery of godliness: God was manifested in the flesh, justified in the Spirit, seen by angels, preached among the Gentiles, believed on in the world, received up in glory. (1 Timothy 3:16)

You search the Scriptures, for in them you think you have eternal life; and these are they which testify of Me. (John 5:39)

For in Him dwells all the fullness of the Godhead bodily. (Colossians 2:9)

Now there was a man in their synagogue with an unclean spirit. And he cried out, saying, "Let us alone! What have we to do with You, Jesus of Nazareth? Did You come to destroy us? I know who You are—the Holy One of God!" But Jesus rebuked him, saying, "Be quiet and come out of him!" (Mark 1:23–25)

For unto us a Child is born, unto us a Son is given; and the government will be upon His shoulder. And His name will be called Wonderful, Counselor, Mighty God, Everlasting Father, Prince of Peace. Of the increase of His government and peace there will be no end, upon the throne of David and over His kingdom, to order it and establish it with judgment and justice from that time forward, even forever. The zeal of the Lord of host will perform this. (Isaiah 9:6–7)

Philip said to Him, "Lord, show us the Father, and it is sufficient for us." Jesus said to him, "Have I been with you so long, and yet you have not known Me, Philip? He who has seen Me has seen the Father; so how can you say, 'Show us the Father'? Do you not believe that I am in the Father, and the Father in Me? The words that I speak to you I do not speak on My own authority; but the Father who dwells in Me does the works. Believe Me that I am in the Father land the Father in Me, or else believe Me for the sake of the works themselves." (John 14:8–11)

Jesus said to him, "I am the way, the truth, and the life. No one comes to the Father except through Me. If you had known Me, you would have known My Father also and from now on you know Him and have seen Him." (John 14:6–7)

And seeing the multitudes, He went up on a mountain, and when He was seated His disciples came to him. Then He opened His mouth and taught them, saying: "Blessed are the poor in spirit, for theirs is the kingdom of heaven. Blessed are those who mourn, for they shall be comforted. Blessed are the meek, For they shall inherit the earth. Blessed are those who hunger and thirst for righteousness, for they shall be filled. Blessed are the merciful, for they shall obtain mercy. Blessed are the pure in heart, for they shall see God. Blessed are the peacemakers, for they shall be called sons of God. Blessed are those who are persecuted for righteousness' sake, for theirs is the kingdom of heaven. Blessed are you when they revile and persecute you, and say all kinds of evil against you falsely for My sake. Rejoice and be exceedingly glad, for great is your reward in heaven, for so they persecuted the prophets who were before you. You are the salt of the earth; but if the salt loses its flavor, how shall it be seasoned? It is then good for nothing but to be thrown out and trampled underfoot by men. You are the light of the world. A city that is set on a hill cannot be hidden. Nor do they light a lamp and put it under a basket, but on a lamp stand, and it gives light to all who are in the house, let your light so shine before men, that they may see your good works and glorify your Father in heaven. Do not think that I came to destroy the Law or the Prophets but to fulfill. For assuredly, I say to you, till heaven and earth pass away, one jot or one tittle will by no means pass from the law till all is fulfilled. Whoever therefore breaks one of the least of these commandments, and teaches men so, shall be called least in the kingdom of heaven; but whoever does and teaches them, he shall be called great in the kingdom of heaven. For I say to you, that unless your righteousness exceeds the righteousness of the scribe and Pharisees, you will by no means enter the kingdom of heaven. You have heard that it was said to those of old, 'You shall not murder, and whoever murders will be in danger the judgment.' But I say to you that whoever is angry with his brother without a cause shall be in danger of the judgment.

"And whoever says to his brother 'Raca!' Shall be in danger of the council. But whoever says, 'You fool!' Shall be in danger of hell fire. Therefore if you bring your gift to the altar, and there remember that your brother has something against you, leave your gift there before the altar, and go your way. First be reconciled to your brother, and then come and offer your gift. Agree with your adversary quickly, while you are on the way with him, lest your adversary deliver you to the judge, the judge hand you over to the officer, and you be thrown into prison. Assuredly, I say to you, you will by no means get out of there till you have paid the last penny. You have heard that it was said to those of old, 'You shall not commit adultery.' But I say to you that whoever looks at a woman to lust for her has already committed adultery with her in his heart. If your right eye cause you to sin, pluck it out and cast it from you; for it is more profitable for you that one of your members perish, than for your whole body to be cast into hell. And if your right hand causes you to sin, cut it off and cast it from you; for it is more profitable for you that one of your members perish, than for your whole body to be cast into hell. Furthermore it has been said, 'Whoever divorces his wife, let him give her a certificate of divorce.' But I say to you that whoever divorces his wife for any reason except sexual immorality causes her to commit adultery; and whoever marries a woman who is divorced commits adultery. Again you have heard that it was said to those of old, 'You shall not swear falsely, but shall perform your oaths to the Lord.' But I say to you, do not swear at all: neither by heaven, for it is God's throne; nor by the earth, for it is His footstool; nor by Jerusalem, for it is the city of the great King. Nor shall you swear by your head, because you cannot make one hair white or black. But let your 'Yes' be 'Yes,' and your 'No,' 'No.' For whatever is more than these is from the evil one. You have heard that it was said, 'An eye for an eye and a tooth for a tooth.' But tell you not to resist an evil person. But whoever slaps you on your right cheek, turn the other to him also. If anyone wants to sue you and take away your tunic, let him have your cloak also. And whoever compels you to go one mile, go with him two. Give to him who asks you, and from him who wants to borrow from you do not turn away. You have heard that it was said, 'You shall love your neighbor and hate your enemy.' But I say to you, love your enemies, bless those who curse you, do good to those who hate you, and pray for those who spitefully use you and persecute you, that you may be sons of your Father in heaven; for He makes His sun rise on the evil and on the good, and sends rain on the just and on the unjust. For if you love those who love you, what reward have you? Do not even the tax collectors do the same? And if you greet your brethren only, what do you do more than others? Do not even the tax collectors do so? Therefore you shall be perfect, just as your Father in heaven's perfect." (Matthew 5:1–48)

My little children, these things I write to you, so that you may not sin. And if anyone sins, we have an Advocate with the Father, Jesus Christ the righteous and He Himself is the propitiation for our sins, and not for ours only but also for the whole world. Now by this we know that we know Him, if we keep His commandments. He who says, "I know Him," and does not keep His commandments, is a liar, and the truth is not in him. But whoever keeps His word, truly the love of God is perfected in him. By this we know that we are in Him. He who says he abides in Him ought himself also to walk just as

He walked. Brethren, I write no new commandment to you, but an old commandment which you have had from the beginning. The old commandment is the word which you heard from the beginning. Again, a new commandment I write to you, which thing is true in Him and in you, because the darkness is passing away, and the true light is already shining. He who says he is in the light, and hates his brother, is in darkness until now. He who loves his brother abides in the light, and there is no cause for stumbling in him. But he who hates his brother is in darkness and walks in darkness, and does not know where he is going, because the darkness has blinded his eyes. I write to you, little children, because your sins are forgiven you for His name's sake. I write to you, fathers, because you have known Him who is from the beginning. I write to you, young men, because you have overcome the wicked one. I write to you, little children, because you have known the Father.

I have written to you, fathers, because you have known Him who is from the beginning. I have written to you, young men, because you are strong, and the word of God abides in you, and you have overcome the wicked one. Do not love the world or the things in the world. If anyone loves the world, the love of the Father is not in him. For all that is in the world the lust of the flesh, the lust of the eyes, and the pride of life—is not the Father but is of the world. And the world is passing away, and the lust of it; but he who does the will of God abides forever. Little children, it is the last hour; and as you have heard that the Antichrists is coming, even now many antichrists have come, by which we know that it is the last hour. They went out from us, but they were not of us; for if they had been of us, they would have continued us; but they went out that they might be made manifest, that none of them whereof us. But you have an anointing from the Holy one, and you know all things. I have not written to you because you do not know the truth, but because you know it, and that no lie is of the truth. Who is a liar but he who denies that Jesus is Christ? He is antichrist who denies the Father and the Son. Whoever denies the Son does not have the Father either; he who acknowledges the Son has the Father also. Therefore let that abide in you which you heard from the beginning. If what you heard from the beginning abides in you, you also will abide in the Son and in the Father. And this is the promise that He has promised us— eternal life. These things I have written to you concerning those who try to deceive you. But the anointing which you have received from Him abides in you, and you do not need that anyone teach you; but as the same anointing teaches you concerning all things, and is true, and is not a lie, and just as it has taught you, you will abide in Him and now, little children, abide in Him, that when He appears, we may have confidence and not be ashamed before Him at His coming. If you know that He is righteous, you know that everyone who practices righteousness is born of Him. (1 John 2:1–29)

Now it came to pass, as He was praying in a certain place, when He ceased, that one of the disciples said to Him, "Lord, teach us to pray, as John also taught his disciples." So He said to them, "When you pray, say, Our Father in heaven, hallowed be Your name. Your kingdom come. Your will be done On earth as it is in heaven. Give us day by day our daily bread. And forgive us our sins, for we also forgive everyone who is indebted to us. And do not lead us into temptation, but deliver us from the evil one." (Luke 11:1–4)

For even the Son of Man did not come to be served but to serve, and to give His life a ransom for many. (Mark 10:45)

And Jesus answered and spoke to them again by parables and said: "The kingdom of heaven is like a certain king who arranged a marriage for his son, and sent out his servants to call those who were invited to the wedding; and they were not willing to come. Again, he sent out other servants, saying, 'Tell those who are invited, "See, I have prepared my dinner; my oxen and fatted cattle are killed, and all things are ready. Come to the wedding."' But they made light of it and went their ways, one his own farm, another to his business. And the rest seized his servants, treated them spitefully, and killed them. But when the king heard about it, he was furious. And he sent out his armies, destroyed those murderers, and burned up their city. Then he said to his servant, 'The weddings ready, but those who were invited were not worthy. Therefore go into the highways, and as many as you find, invite to the wedding.' So those servants went out into the highways and gathered together all whom they found, both bad and good. And the wedding hall was filled with guests. But when the king came in to see the guests he saw a man there who did not have on a wedding garment. So he said to him, 'Friend, how did you come in here without a wedding garment?' And he was speechless. Then the king said to the servants, 'Bind him hand and foot, take him away, and cast him into outer darkness; there will be weeping and gnashing of teeth.' For many are called, but few are chosen."

Then the Pharisees went and plotted how they might entangle Him in His talk. And they sent to Him their disciples with the Herodians, saying, "Teacher, we know that You are true, and teach the way of God in truth; nor do You care about anyone, for You do not regard the person of men. Tell us, therefore, what do You think? Is it lawful to pay taxes to Caesar, or not?"

But Jesus perceived their wickedness and said, "Why do you test Me you hypocrites? Show Me the tax money." So they brought Him a denarius. And He said to them, "Whose image and inscription is this?" They said to Him, "Caesar's." And He said to them, "Render therefore to Caesar the things that are Caesar's and to God the things that are God's." When they had heard these words, they marveled, and left Him and went their way.

The same day the Sadducees, who say there is no resurrection, came to Him and asked Him, saying: "Teacher, Moses said that if a man dies, having no children, his brother shall marry his wife and raise up offspring for his brother. Now there were with us seven brothers. The first died after he had married, and having no offspring, left his wife to his brother. Likewise the second also, and the third, even to the seventh. Last of all the woman died also. Therefore, in the resurrection, whose wife of the seven will she be? For they

## JESUS IS GOD

all had her." Jesus answered and said to them, "You are mistaken, not knowing the Scriptures nor the power of God. For in the resurrection they neither marry nor are given in marriage, but are like angels of God in heaven. But concerning the resurrection of the dead, have you not read what was spoken to you by God, saying, 'I am the God of Abraham, the God of Isaac, and the God of Jacob'? God is not the God of the dead, but of the living." And when the multitudes heard this they were astonished at His teaching. But when the Pharisees heard that He had silenced the Sadducees, they gathered together. Then one of them, a lawyer, asked Him a question, testing Him, and saying, "Teacher, which is the great commandment in the law?" Jesus said to him, "'You shall love the Lord your God with all your heart, with all your soul, and with all your mind.' This is the first and great commandment. And the second is like it: 'You shall love your neighbor as yourself.' On these two commandments hang all the Law and the Prophets."

While the Pharisees were gathered together, Jesus asked them, saying, "What do you think about the Christ? Whose Son is He?" They said to Him, "The Son of David." He said to them, "How then does David in the Spirit call Him Lord, saying: 'The Lord said to my Lord, "Sit at My right hand, till I make Your enemies Your footstool"'? If David then calls Him Lord, how is He his Son?" And no one was able to answer Him a word, nor from that day on did anyone dare question Him anymore. (Matthew 22:1–46)

And again He began to teach by the sea. And a great multitude was gathered to Him, so that He got into a boat and sat in it on the sea; and the whole multitude was on the land facing the sea. Then He taught them many things by parables, and said to them in His teaching: "Listen! Behold, a sower went out to sow. And it happened as he sowed, that some seed fell by the wayside; and the birds of the air came and devoured it. Some fell on stony ground, where it did not have much earth; and immediately it sprang up because it had no depth of earth. But when the sun was up it was scorched, and because it had no root it withered away. And some seed fell among thorns; and the thorns grew up and choked it, and it yielded no crop. But other seed fell on good ground and yielded a crop that sprang up, increased and produced: some thirty, some sixty, and some a hundred." And He said to them, "He who has ears to hear, let him hear!" But when He was alone, those around Him with the twelve asked Him about the parable. And He said to them, "To you it has been given to know the mystery of the kingdom of God; but to those who are outside, all things come in parables, so that 'Seeing they may see and not perceive, and hearing they may hear and not understand; lest they should turn, and their sins be forgiven them.'" And He said to them, "Do you not understand this parable? How then will you understand all the parables? The sower sows the word. And these are the ones by the wayside where the word is sown. When they hear, satan comes immediately and takes away the word that was sown in their hearts.

"These likewise are the ones sown on stony ground who, when they hear the word, immediately receive it with gladness; and they have no root in themselves, and so endure only for a time, Afterward, when tribulation or persecution arises for the world's sake, immediately they stumble. Now these are the ones sown among thorns; they are the ones who hear the word, and the cares of this world, the deceitfulness of riches, and the desires for other things entering in choke the word, and it becomes unfruitful. But these are the ones sown on good ground, those who hear the word, accept it, and bear fruit: some thirty fold, some sixty, and some a hundred."

Also, He said to them, "Is a lamp brought to be put under a basket of under a bed? Is it not to be set on a lamp stand? For there is nothing hidden which will not be revealed, nor has anything been kept secret but that it should come to light. If anyone has ears to hear, let him hear." Then He said to them, "Take heed what you hear. With the same measure you use, it will be measured to you; and to you who hear, more will be given. For whoever has, to him more will be given; but whoever does not have, even what he has will be taken away from him."

And He said, "The kingdom of God is as if a man should scatter seed on ground, and should sleep by night and rise by day, and the seed should spout and grow, he himself does not know how. For the earth yields crops by itself: first the blade, then the head, after that the full grain in the head. But when the grain ripens, immediately he puts in the sickle, because the harvest has come." Then He said, "To what shall we liken the kingdom of God? Or with what parable shall we picture it? It is like a mustard seed which, when it is sown on the ground, is smaller than all the seeds on earth; but when it is sown, it grows up and becomes greater than all herbs, and shoots out large branches, so that the birds of the air may nest under its shade."

And with many such parables He spoke the word to them as they were able to hear it. But without a parables He did not speak to them. And when they were alone, He explained all things to His disciples. (Mark 4:1–34)

When He had called the people to Himself, with His disciples also, He said to them, "Whoever desires to come after Me, let him deny himself, and take up his cross, and follow Me. For whoever desires to save his life will lose it, but whoever loses his life for My sake and the gospel's will save it. For what will it profit a man if he gains the whole world, and loses his own soul? Or what will a man give in exchange for his soul? For whoever is ashamed of Me and My words in this adulterous and sinful generation, of him the Son of Man also will be ashamed when He comes in the glory of His Father with the Holy angels." (Mark 8:34–38)

Then He lifted up His eyes towards His disciples, and said: "Blessed are you poor, for yours is the kingdom of God. Blessed are you who hungered now, for you shall be filled. Blessed are you who weep now, for you shall laugh. Blessed are you when men hate you, and when they exclude you, and revile you, and cast out your name as evil, for the Son of Man's sake. Rejoice in that day and leap for joy! For indeed your reward is great in heaven, for in like manner their fathers did to the prophets. But woe to you who are rich, for you have received your consolation. Woe to you who are full, for you shall hunger. Woe to you who laugh now, for you shall mourn and weep. Woe to you when all men speak well of you, for so did their fathers to the false prophets. But I say to you who hears: love your enemies, do good to those who hate you, bless those who curse you, and pray for those who spitefully use you. To him who strikes you on the one cheek, offer the other also. From him who takes away your cloak, do not withhold your tunic either. Give to everyone who ask of you. And from him who takes away your goods do not ask them back. And just as you want men to do to you, you also do to them likewise. But if you love those who love you, what credit is that to you? For even sinners love those who love them and if you do good to those who do good to you, what credit is that to you? For even sinners the same. And if you lend to those from whom you hope to receive back, what credit is that to you? For even sinners lend to sinners to receive as much back. But love your enemies, do good, and lend, hoping for nothing in return; and your reward will be great, and you will be sons of the Most High, for He is kind to the unthankful and the evil. Therefore, be merciful, just as your Father also is merciful. Judge not, and you shall not be judged. Condemn not, and you shall not be condemned. Forgive, and you will be forgiven. Give, and it will be given to you: good measure, pressed down, shaken together, and running over will be put into your bosom. For with the same measure that you use, it will be measured back to you."

And He spoke a parable to them: "Can the blind lead the blind? Will they not both fall into the ditch? A disciple is not above his teacher, but everyone who is perfectly trained will be like his teacher. And why do you look at the speck in your brother's eye, but do not perceive the plank in your own eye? Or how can you say to your brother, 'Brother, let me remove the speck that is in your eye.' When you yourself do not see the plank that is in your own eye? Hypocrite! First remove the plank from your own eye, and then you will see clearly to remove the speck that is in your brother's eye. For a good tree does not bear bad fruit, nor does a bad tree bear good fruit. For every tree is known by its own fruit. For men do not gather figs from thorns, nor do they gather grapes from a bramble bush. A good man out of the good treasure of his heart brings forth good; and an evil man out of the evil treasure of his heart brings forth evil. For out of the abundance of the heart his mouth speaks. But why do you call Me 'Lord, Lord' and not do the things which I say? Whoever comes to Me, and hears My sayings and does them, will show you whom he is like: He is like a man building a house, who dug deep and laid the foundation on a rock. And when the flood arose, the stream beat vehemently against that house, and could not shake it, for it was founded on the rock. But he who heard and did nothing is like a man who built a house on the earth without a foundation, against which the stream beat vehemently; and immediately it fell. And the ruin of that house was great." (Luke 6:20–49)

In the meantime, when an innumerable multitude of people had gathered together, so that they trampled one another, He began to say to His disciples first of all, "Beware of the leaven

## JESUS IS GOD

of the Pharisees, which is hypocrisy for there is nothing covered that will not be revealed, nor hidden that will not be known. Therefore, whatever you have spoken in the dark will be heard in the light, and what you have spoken in the ear in inner rooms will be proclaimed on the housetops. And I say to you, My friends, do not be afraid of those who kill the body, and after that have no more that they can do. But I will show you whom you should fear: Fear Him who, after He has killed, has power to cast into hell; yes I say to you, fear Him! Are not five sparrows sold for two copper coins? And not one of them is forgotten before God. But the very hairs of your head are numbered. Do not fear therefore; you are of more value than many sparrows. Also I say to you, whoever confesses Me before men, him the Son of Man also will confess before the angels of God. But he who denies Me before men will be denied before the angels of God. And anyone who speaks a word against the Son of Man, it will be forgiven him; but to him who blasphemes against the Holy Spirit, it will not be forgiven. Now when they bring you to the synagogues and magistrates and authorities, do not worry about how or what you should answer, or what you should say. For the Holy Spirit will teach you in that very hour what you ought to say."

Then one from the crowd said to Him, "Teacher, tell my brother to divide the inheritance with me." But He said to him, "Man, who made Me a judge or an arbitrator over you?" And He said to them, "Take heed and beware of covetousness. for one's life does not consist in the abundance of things he possesses." Then He spoke a parable to them, saying: "The ground of certain rich man yielded plentifully. And he thought within himself, saying, 'What shall I do, since I have no room to store my crops?' So he said, 'I will do this: I will pull down my barns and build greater, and there I will store all my crops and my goods. And I will say to my soul, 'Soul you have many goods laid up for many years; take your ease; eat drink, and be merry,' But God said to him, 'Fool! This night your soul will be required of you; then whose will those things be which you have provided?' So is he who lays up treasure for himself, and is not rich toward God."

Then He said to His disciples, "Therefore I say to you, do not worry about your life, what you will eat; nor about the body, what you will put on. Life is more than food, and the body is more than clothing. Consider the ravens, for they neither sow nor reap, which have neither storehouse nor barn; and God feeds them. Of how much more value are you than the birds? And which of you by worrying can add on cubit to his stature? If you then are not able to do the least, why are you anxious for the rest? Consider the lilies, how they grow: they neither toil nor spin; and yet I say to you, even Solomon in all his glory was not arrayed like one of these. If then God so clothes the grass, which today is in the field and tomorrow is thrown into the oven, how much more will He clothe you, O you of little faith? And do not seek what you should eat or what you should drink, nor have an anxious mind. For all these things the nations of the world seek after, and your Father knows that you need these things. But seek the kingdom of God, and all these things shall be added to you. Do not fear, little flock, for it is your Father's good pleasure to give you the kingdom. Sell what you have and give alms; provide yourselves many bags which do not grow old, a treasure in the heavens that does not fail, where no thief approaches nor moth destroys. For where your treasure is, there your heart will be also. Let your waist be girded and your lamps burning; and you yourselves be like men who wait for their master, when he will return from the wedding, that when he comes and knocks they may open to him immediately. Blessed are those servants whom the master, when he comes, will find watching. Assuredly, I say to you that he will grid himself and have them sit down to eat, and will come and serve them. And if he should come in the second watch, or come in the third watch, and find them so blessed are those servants. But know this, that if the master of the house had known what hour the thief would come, he would have watched and not allowed his house to be broken into. Therefore you also be ready, for the Son of Man is coming at an hour you do not expect." Then Peter said to Him, "Lord, do You speak this parable only to us, or to all people?" And the Lord said, "Who then is that faithful and wise steward, whom his master will make ruler over his household, to give them their portion of food in due season? Blessed is that servant whom his master will find so doing when he comes. Truly, I say to you that he will make him ruler over all that he has. But if that servant says in his heart, 'My master is delaying his coming,' and begins to beat the male and female servants, and to eat and drink and be drunk, the master of that servant will come on a day when he is not looking for him, and at an hour when he is not aware, and will cut him in two and appoint him his portion with the unbelievers. And that servant who knew his master's will, and did not prepare himself or do according to his will, shall be beaten with many stripes. But he who did not know, yet committed things deserving of stripes, shall be beaten with few. For everyone to whom much is given, from him much will be required; and to whom much has been committed, of him they will ask the more. I came to send fire on the earth, and how I wish it were already kindled! But I have a baptism to be baptized with, and how distressed I am till it is accomplished! Do you suppose that I came to give peace on earth? I tell you, not at all, but rather division. For from now on five in one house will be divided: three against two, and two against three. Father will be divided against son and son against father, mother against daughter and daughter against mother, mother-in-law and daughter-in-law against her mother-in-law."

Then He also said to the multitudes, "Whenever you see a cloud rising out of the west, immediately you say, 'A shower is coming'; and so it is. And when you see the south wind blow, you say, 'There will be hot weather'; and there is. Hypocrites! You can discern the face of the sky and of the earth, but how is it you do not discern this time? Yes, and why, even of yourselves, do you not judge what is right? When you go with your adversary to the magistrate, make every effort along the way to settle with him, last he drag you to the judge, the judge deliver you to the officer, and the officer throw you into prison. I tell you, you shall not depart from there till you have paid the very last mite." (Luke 12:1–59)

## JESUS IS GOD

After this there was a feast of the Jews, and Jesus went up to Jerusalem. Now there is in Jerusalem by the Sheep Gate a pool, which is called in Hebrew, Bethesda, having five porches. In these lay a great multitude of sick people, blind, lame, paralyzed, waiting for the moving of the water, for an angel went down at a certain time into the pool and stirred up the water; then whoever stepped in first, after the stirring of the water, was made well of whatever disease he had. Now a certain man was there who had an infirmity thirty-eight years. When Jesus saw him lying there, and knew that he already had been in that condition long time, He said to him, "Do you want to be made well?" The sick man answer Him, "Sir, I have no man to put me into the pool when the water is stirred up; but while I am coming, another steps down before me." Jesus said to him, "Rise, take up your bed and walk." And immediately the man was made well, took up his bed, and walked. And that day was the Sabbath. The Jews therefore said to him who was cured, "It is the Sabbath; it is not lawful for you to carry your bed." He answered them, "He who made me well said to me, 'Take up your bed and walk.'" Then they asked him, "Who is the Man who said to you, 'Take up your bed and walk'?" But the one who was healed did not know who it was, for Jesus had withdrawn, a multitude being in that place. After Jesus found him in the temple and said to him, "See, you have been made well. Sin no more, lest a worse thing come upon you." The man departed and told the Jews that it was Jesus who had made him well. For this reason the Jews persecuted Jesus and sought to kill Him, because He had done these things on the Sabbath.

But Jesus answered them, "My Father has been working until now, and I have been working." Therefore the Jews sought all the more to kill Him, because He not only broke the Sabbath, but also said that God was His Father, making Himself equal with God. Then Jesus answered and said to them, "Most assuredly, I say to you, the Son can do nothing of Himself, but what He sees the Father do; for whatever He does, the Son also does in like manner. For the Father loves the Son, and Shows Him all things that He Himself does; and He will show Him greater works than these, that you may marvel. For as the Father raises the dead and gives life to them, even so the Son gives life to whom He will. For the Father judges no one, but has committed all judgment to the Son, that all should honor the Son just as they honor the Father. He who does not honor the Son does not honor the Father who sent Him. Most assuredly, I say to you, he who hears My word and believes in Him who sent Me has everlasting life, and shall not come into judgement, but has passed from death into life. Most assuredly, I say to you, the hour is coming, and now is, when the dead will hear the voice of the Son of God; and those who hear will live. For as the Father has life in Himself, so He has granted the Son to have life in Himself, and has given Him authority to execute judgement also, because He is the Son of Man. Do not marvel at this; for the hour is coming in which all who are in the graves will hear His voice and come forth—those who have done good, to the resurrection of life, and those who have done evil, to the resurrection of condemnation. I can of Myself do nothing. As I hear, I judge; and My judgment is righteous, because I do not seek My own will but the will of the Father who sent Me. If I bear witness of Myself, My witness is not true. There is another who bears witness of Me, and I know that the witness which He witnesses of Me is true. You have sent to John, and he has borne witness to the truth. Yet I do not receive testimony from man, but I say these things that you may be saved. He was the burning and shining lamp, and you were willing a time to rejoice in his light. But I have a greater witness than John for the works which the Fathers given Me to finish—the very works that I do—bear witness of Me, that the Father has sent Me. And the Father Himself, who sent Me, has testified of Me. You have neither heard His voice at any time, nor seen His form. But you do not have His word abiding in you, because whom He sent, Him you do not believe. You teach the Scripture, for in them you think you have eternal life; and these are they which testify of Me. But you are not willing to come to Me that you may have life. I do not receive honor from men. But I know you, that you do not have the love of God in you. I have come in My Father's name, and you do not receive Me; if another comes in his own name, him you will receive.

"How can you believe, who receive honor from one another, and do not seek the honor that comes from the only God? Do not think that I shall accuse you to the Father; there is one who accuses you—Moses, in whom you trust. For if you believed Moses, you would believe Me; for he wrote about Me. But if you do not believe his writings, how will you believe My words?" (John 5:1–47)

Now before the Feast of the Passover, when Jesus knew that His hour had come that He should depart from this world to the Father, having loved His own who were in the world, He loved them to the end. And supper being ended, the devil having already put it into the heart of Judas Iscariot, Simon's son, to betray Him, Jesus, knowing that the Father had given all things into His hands, and that He had come from God and was going to God, rose from supper and laid aside His garments, took a towel and girded Himself. After that He poured water into a basin and began to wash the disciples' feet, and to wipe them with the towel with which He was girded. Then he came to Simon Peter. And Peter said to Him, "Lord, are You washing my feet?" Jesus answered and said to him, "What I am doing you do not understand now, but you will know after this." Peter said to Him, "You shall never wash my feet!" Jesus answered him, "If I do not wash you, you have no part with Me." Simon Peter said to Him, "Lord, not my feet only, but also my hands and my head!" Jesus said to him, "He who is bathed needs only to wash his feet, but is completely clean; and you are clean, but not all of you." For He knew who would betray Him; therefore He said, "You are not all clean." So when He had washed their feet, taken His garments, and sat down again, He said to them, "Do you know what I have done to you? You call Me Teacher and Lord, and you say well, for so I am. If I then, your Lord and Teacher, have washed your feet, you also ought to wash one another's feet. For I have given you an example, that you should do as I have done to you. Most assuredly, I say to you, a servant is not greater than his master; nor is he who is sent greater than he who sent him. If you know these things, blessed are you if you do them. I do not seek concerning all of you. I know whom I have chosen; but that the Scripture may be fulfilled, He who eats bread with Me has lifted up his heel against Me. Now I tell you before it comes, that when it does come to pass, you may believe that I am He. Most assuredly, I say to you, he who receives whoever I send receives Me; and he who receives Me receives Him who sent Me."* When Jesus had said these things, He was troubled in spirit, and testified and said, *"Most assuredly, I say to you, one of you will betray Me."* Then the disciples looked at one another, perplexed about whom He spoke. Now there was leaning on Jesus bosom one of His disciples, whom Jesus loved. Simon Peter therefore motioned to him to ask who it was of whom He spoke. Then, leaning back on Jesus breast, he said to Him, "Lord, who is it?" Jesus answered, *"It is he to whom I shall give a piece of bread when I have dipped it."* And having dipped the bread, He gave it to Judas Iscariot, the son of Simon. Now after the piece of bread, Satan entered him. Then Jesus said to him, *"What you do, do quickly."* But no one at the table knew for what reason He said this to him. For some thought, because Judas had the money box, that Jesus had said to him, "Buy those things we need for the feast," or that he should give something to the poor. Having received the piece of bread, he then went out immediately. And it was night. So, when he had gone out, Jesus said, *"Now the Son of Man is glorified, and God is glorified in Him. If God is glorified in Him, God will also glorify Him Himself, and glorify Him immedi-*

ately. Little children, I shall be with you a little while longer. You will seek Me; and as I said to the Jews, 'Where I am going, you cannot come,' so now I say to you. A new commandment I give to you, that you love one another; as I have loved you, that you also love one another. Buy this all will know that you are My disciples, if you have love for one another." Simon Peter said to Him, "Lord, where are You going?" Jesus answered him, "Where I am going you cannot follow Me now, but you shall follow Me afterward." Peter said to Him, Lord, why can I not follow You now? Will lay down my life for Your sake." Jesus answered him, "Will you lay down your life for My sake? Most assuredly, I say to you, the rooster shall not crow till you have denied Me three times." (John 13:1–37)

"Let not your heart be troubled; you believe in God, believe also in Me. In My Father house are many mansions; if it were not so, I would have told you. I go to prepare a place for you. And if I go and prepare a place for you, I will come again and receive you to Myself; that where I am, there you may be also. And where I go you know, and the way you know." Thomas said to Him, "Lord, we do not know where You are going, and how can we know the way?" Jesus said to him, "I am the way the truth, and the life. No one comes to the Father except through Me. If you had known Me, you would have known My Father also; and from now on you know Him and have seen Him." Philip said to Him, "Lord, show us the Father, and it is sufficient for us." Jesus said to him, "Have I been with you so long, and yet you have not known Me, Philip? He who has seen Me has seen the Father; so how can you say, 'Show us the Father'? Do you not believe that I am in the Father, and the Father in Me? The words that I speak to you I do not speak on My own authority; but the Father who dwells in Me does the works. Believe Me that I am in the Father and the Father in Me, or else believe Me for the sake of the works themselves. And whatever you ask in My name, that Will do, that the Father may be glorified in the Son. If you ask anything in My name I will do it. If you love Me, keep My commandments. And I will pray the Father, and He will give you another Helper, that He may abide with you forever—the Spirit of Truth, whom the world cannot receive, because it neither sees Him nor knows Him; but you know Him, for He dwells with you and will be in you. I will not leave you orphans; I will come to you. A little while longer and the world wills Me no more, but you will see Me. Because I live, you will live also. At that day you will know that I am in My Father, and you in Me, and I in you. He who has My commandments and keeps them, it is he who loves Me. And he who loves Me will be loved by My Father, and I will love him and manifest Myself to him." Judas (not Iscariot) said to Him, "Lord how is it that You will manifest Yourself to us, and not to the world?" Jesus answered and said to him, "If anyone loves Me, he will keep My word; and My Father will love him, and We will come to him and make Our home with him. He who does not love Me does not keep My words; and the word which you hear is not Mine but the Father's who sent Me. These things I have spoken to you while being present with you. But the Helper, the Holy Spirit, whom the Father will send in My name, He will teach you all things and bring to your remembrance all things that I said to you. Peace I leave with you, My peace I give to you; not as the world gives do I give to you. Let not your heart be troubled, neither let it be afraid. You have heard Me say to you 'I am going away and coming back to you.' If you loved Me, you would rejoice because I said, 'I am going to the Father,' for My Father is greater than I. And now I have told you before it comes, that when it does come to pass, you may believe. I will no longer talk much with you, for the ruler of this world is coming, and he has nothing in Me. But that the world may know that I Love the Father, and as the Father gave Me commandment, so I do. Arise, let us go from here." (John 14:1–31)

I am the true vine, and My Father is the vinedresser. Every branch in Me that does not bear fruit He takes away; and every branch that bears fruit He prunes, that it may bear more fruit. You are already clean because of the word which I have spoken to you. Abide in Me, and I in you. As the branch cannot bear fruit of itself, unless it abides in the vine, neither can you, unless you abide in Me. I am the vine, you are the branches. He who abides in Me, and I in him, bears much fruit; for without Me you can do nothing. If anyone does not abide in Me, he is cast out as a branch and is withered; and they gather them and throw them into the fire, and they are burned. If you abide in Me, and My words abide in you, you will ask what you desire, and it shall be done for you. By this My Father is glorified, that you bear much fruit; so you will be

My disciples, as the Father loved Me, I also have loved you; abide in My love. If you keep My commandments, you will abide in My love, just as I have kept My Father's commandments and abide in His love. These things I have spoken to you, that My joy may remain in you, and that your joy may be full. This is My commandment, that you love one another as I have loved you.

Greater love has no one than this, than to lay down one's life for his friends. You are My friends if you do whatever I command you. No longer do I call you servants, for a servant does not know what his master is doing; but I have called you friends, for all things that I heard from My Father I have made known to you. You did not choose Me, but I chose you and appointed you that you should go and bear fruit, and that your fruit should remain, that whatever you ask the Father in My name He may give you. These things I command you, that you love one another. If the world hates you, you know that it hated Me before it hated you. If you were of the world, the world would love its own. Yet because you are not of the world, but I chose you out of the world, therefore the world hates you. Remember the word that I said to you, "A servant is not greater than his master." If they persecuted Me, they will also persecute you. If they kept My word, they will keep yours also. But all these things they will do to you for My name's sake, because they do not know Him who sent Me. If I had not come and spoken to them, they would have no sin, but now they have no excuse for their sin. He who hates Me hates My Father also. If I had not done among them the works which no one else did, they would have no sin; but now they have seen and also hated both Me and My Father. But this happened that the word might be fulfilled which is written in their law, "There hated Me without a cause." But when the Helper comes, whom I shall send to you from the Father, the Spirit of truth who proceeds from the Father, He will testify of Me. And you also will bear witness, because you have been with Me from the beginning. (John 15:1–27)

"These things I have spoken to you, that you should not be made to stumble. They will put you out of the synagogues; yes, the time is coming that whoever kills you will think that he offers God service. And these things they will do to you because they have not known the Father nor Me. But these things I have told you, that when the time comes, you may remember that I told you of them. And these things I did not say to you at the beginning, because I was with you. But now I go away to Him who sent Me, and none of you asks Me, "Where are You going?" But because I have said these things to you, sorrow has filled your heart. Nevertheless, I tell you the truth. It is to your advantage that I go away; for if I do not go away, the Helper will not come to you; but if I depart, I will send Him to you. And when He has come, He will convict the world of sin, and of righteousness, and judgment: of sin, because they do not believe in Me; of righteousness, because I go to My Father and you see Me no more; of judgment, because the ruler of this world is judged. to you, but you cannot bear them now. However, when He, the Spirit of truth, has come, He will guide you into all truth; for He will not speak on His own authority, but whatever He hears He will speak; and He will tell you things to come. He will glorify Me, for He will take of what is Mine and declare it to you. All things that the Father has are Mine. Therefore, I said that He will take of Mine and declare it to you. A little while, and you will not see Me, and again a little while, and you will see Me, because I go to the Father."

Then some of His disciples said among themselves, "What's this that He says to us, 'A little while, and you will not see Me; and again a little while, and you will see Me'; and 'Because I go to the Father'?" They said therefore, "What is this that He says, 'A little while'? We do not know what He is saying."

Now Jesus knew that they desired to ask Him, and He said to them, "Are you inquiring among yourselves about what I said, 'A little while, and you will not see Me; and again a little while, and you will see Me'? Most assuredly, I say to you that that you will weep and lament, but the world will rejoice; and you will be sorrowful, but your sorrow will be turned into joy. A woman, when she is in labor, has sorrow because her hour has come; but as soon as she has given birth to the child, she no longer remembers the anguish, for joy that a human being has been born into the world. Therefore, you now have sorrow; but I will see you again and your heart will rejoice, and your joy no one will take from you. And in that day you will ask Me nothing. Most assuredly, I say to you, whatever you ask the Father in My name He will give you. Until now you have asked nothing in My name. Ask, and you will receive, that your joy may be full.

"These things I have spoken to you in figurative language; but the time is coming when I will no longer speak to you in figurative language, but I will tell you plainly about the Father. In that day you will ask in My name, and I do not say to you that I shall pray the Father for you; for the Father Himself loves you, because you have loved Me, and have believed that I came forth from God. I came forth from the Father and have come into the world. Again, I leave the world and go to the Father."

His disciples said to Him, "See, now You are speaking plainly, and using no figure of speech! Now we are sure that You know all things, and have no need that anyone should question You. By this we believe that You came forth from God."

Jesus answered them, "Do you now believe? Indeed, the hour is coming, yes, has now come, that you will be scattered, each to his own, and will leave Me alone. And yet I am not alone, because the Father is with Me. These things I have spoken to you, that in Me you may have peace. In the world you will have tribulation; but be of good cheer, I have overcome the world." (John 16:1–33)

Jesus spoke these words, lifted up His eyes to heaven, and said: "Father, the hour has come. Glorify Your Son, that Your Son also may glorify You, as You have given Him authority over all flesh, that He should give eternal life as many as You have given Him. And this is eternal life, that they may know You, the only true God, and Jesus Christ whom You have sent. I have glorified You on earth. I have finished the work which You have given Me to do. And now, O Father, glorify Me together with Yourself, with the glory which I had with You before the world was. I have manifested Your name to the men whom You have given Me out of the world. They were Yours, You gave them to Me, and they have kept Your word. Now they have known that all things which You have given Me are from You. For I have given to them the words which You have given Me; and they have received them, and have known surely that I came forth from You; and they have believed that You sent Me. I pray for them. I do not pray for the world but for those whom You have given Me, for they are Yours. And all Mine are Yours, and Yours are Mine, and I am glorified in them. Now I am no longer in the world, but these are in the world, and I come to You. Holy Father, keep through Your name those whom You have given Me, that they may be one as We are. While I was with them in the world, I kept them in Your name. Those whom You gave Me I have kept; and none of them is lost except the son of perdition, that the Scripture might be fulfilled. But now I come to You, and these things I speak in the world, that they may have My joy fulfilled in themselves. I have given them Your word; and the world has hated them because they are not of the world, just as I am not of the world. I do not pray that You should take them out of the world, but that You should keep them from evil one. They are not of the world, just as I am not of the world. Sanctify them by Your truth. Your word is truth. As You sent Me into the world, I also have sent them into the world. And for their sakes I sanctify Myself, that they also may be sanctified by the truth. I do not pray for these alone, but also for those who will believe in Me through their word; that they all may be one, as You, Father, are in Me, and I in You; that they also may be one in Us, that the world may believe that You sent Me. And the glory which You gave Me I have given them, that they may be one just as We are one: I in them, and You in Me; that they may be made perfect in one, and that the world may know that You have sent Me, and have loved them as You have loved Me. Father, I desire that they also whom You gave Me may be with Me where I am, that they may behold My glory which You have given Me; for You loved Me before the foundation of the world. O righteous Father! The world has not known You, but I have known You; and these have known that You sent Me. And I have declared to them Your name, and will declare it, that the love with which You loved Me may be in them, and I in them." (John 17:1–26)

Take heed that you do not do your charitable deeds before men, to be seen by them. Otherwise, you have no reward from your Father in heaven. Therefore, when you do a charitable deed, do not sound a trumpet before you as the hypocrite do in the synagogues and in the streets, that they may have glory from men. Assuredly, I say to you, They have their reward. But when you do a charitable deed, do not let your left hand know what your right hand is doing, that your charitable deed may be in secret; and your Father who sees in secret will Himself reward you openly. And when you pray, you shall not be like the hypocrites. For they love to pray standing in the synagogues and on the corners of the street, that they may be seen by men. Assuredly, I say to you, they have their reward. But you, when you pray, go into your room, and when you have shut your door, pray to your Father who is in the secret place; and your Father who sees in secret will reward you openly. And when you pray, do not use vain repetitions as the heathen do. For they think that they will be heard for their many words. Therefore do not be like them. For your Father knows the things you have need of before you ask Him. In this manner, therefore, pray; Our Father in heaven, hallowed be Your name. Your kingdom come. Your will be done on earth as it is heaven. Give us this day our daily bread. And forgive us our debts, As we forgive our debtors. And do not lead us into temptation, But deliver us from the evil one. For Yours is the kingdom and the power and the glory forever. Amen. For if you forgive men their trespasses, your heavenly Father will also forgive you. But if you do not forgive men their trespasses, neither will your Father forgive your trespasses. Moreover, when you fast, do not be like the hypocrites, with a sad countenance. For they disfigure their faces that they may appear to men to be fasting. Assuredly, I say to you, they have their reward. But you, when you fast, anoint your head and wash your face, so that you do not appear to men to be fasting, but to your Father who is in the secret place; and your Father who sees in secret will reward you openly. Do not lay up for yourselves treasures on earth, where moth and rust destroy and where thieves break in and steal; but lay up for yourselves treasures in heaven, where neither moth nor rust destroys and where thieves do not break I and steal. For where your treasure is, there your heart will be also. The lamp of the body is the eye. If therefore your eye is good, your whole body will be full of light. But if your eye is bad, your whole body will be full of darkness. If therefore the light that is in you is darkness, how great is that darkness! No one can serve two masters; for either he will hate the one and love the other, or else he will be loyal to the one and despise the other. You cannot serve God and mammon. Therefore I say to you, do not worry about your life, what you will eat or what you will drink; nor about your body, what you will put on. Is not life more than food and the body more than clothing? Look at the birds of the air, for they neither sow nor reap nor gather into barns; yet your heavenly Father feeds them. Are you not of more value than they? Which of you by worrying can add one cubit to his stature? So why do you worry about clothing? Consider the lilies of the field, how they grow: they neither toil nor spin; and yet I say to you that even Solomon in all his glory was not arrayed like one of these. Now if God so clothes the grass of the field, which today is, and tomorrow is thrown into the oven, will He not much more clothe you, O you of little faith? Therefore do not worry, saying "What shall we eat?" or "What shall we drink?" or "What shall we wear?" For after all these things the Gentiles seek. For your heavenly Father knows that you need all these things, but seek first the kingdom of God and His righteousness, and all these things shall be added to you. Therefore, do not worry about tomorrow, for tomorrow will worry about its own things. Sufficient for the day is its own trouble. (Matthew 6:1–34)

"Judge not, that you be not judged. For with what judgment you judge, you will be judged; and with the measure you use, it will be measured back to you. And why do you look at the speck in your brother's eye, but do not consider the plank in your own eye? Or how can you say to your brother, 'Let me remove the speck from your eye'; and look, a plank is in your own eye? Hypocrite! First remove the plank from your own eye, and then you will see clearly to remove the speck from your brother's eye. Do not give what is holy to the dogs; nor cast your pearls before swine, lest they trample them under their feet, and turn and tear you in pieces.

"Ask, and it will be given to you; seek, and you will find; knock, and it will be opened to you. For everyone who asks receives, and he who seeks finds, and to him who knocks it will be opened. Or what man is there among you who, if his son asks for bread, will give him a stone? Or if he asks for a fish, will he give him a serpent? If you then, being evil, know how to give good gifts to your children, how much more will your Father who is in heaven give good things to those who ask Him! Therefore, whatever you want men to do to you, do also to them, for this is the Law and the Prophets. Enter by the narrow gate; for wide is the gate and broad is the way that leads to destruction, and there are many who go in by it. Because narrow is the gate and difficult is the way which leads to life, and there are few who find it. Beware of false prophets, who come to you in sheep's clothing, but inwardly they are ravenous wolves, You will know them by their fruits. Do men gather grapes from thorn bushes or figs from thistles? Even so, every good tree bears good fruit, but a bad tree bears bad fruit. A good tree cannot bear bad fruit, nor can a bad tree bear good fruit. Every tree that does not bear good fruit is cut down and thrown into the fire. Therefore by their fruits you will know them. Not everyone who says to Me, 'Lord, Lord,' shall enter the kingdom of heaven, but he who does the will of My Father in heaven. Many will say to Me in that day, 'Lord, Lord, have we not prophesied in Your name, cast out demons in Your name, and done many wonders in Your name?' And then I will declare to them, 'I never knew you; depart from Me, you who practice lawlessness!' Therefore, whoever hears these sayings of Mine, and does them, I will liken him to a wise man who built his house on the rock: and the rain descended, the floods came, and the winds blew and beat on that house; and it did not fall for it was founded on the rock. But everyone who hears these sayings of Mine, and does not do them, will be like a foolish man who built his house on the sand: and the rain descended, the floods came, and the winds blew and beat on that house; and it fell. And great was its fall."

And so it was, when Jesus had ended these sayings, that the people were astonished at His teaching, for He taught them as one having authority, and not as the scribes. (Matthew 7:1–29)

And when He had called His twelve disciples to Him, He gave them power over unclean spirits, to cast them out, and to heal all kinds of sickness and all kinds of disease. Now the names of the twelve apostles are these: first, Simon, who is called Peter, and Andrew his brother;

James the son of Zebedee, and John his brother; Philip and Bartholomew; Thomas and Matthew the tax collector; James the son of Alphas, and Lebbaeus, whose surname was Thaddeus; Simon the Canaanite, and Judas Iscariot, who also betrayed Him. These twelve Jesus sent out and commanded them, saying: "Do not go into the way of the Gentiles, and do not enter a city of the Samaritans. But go rather to the lost sheep of the house of Israel. And as you go, preach, saying, 'The kingdom of heaven is at hand.' Heal the sick, cleanse the lepers, raise the dead, cast out demons. Freely you have received, freely give. Provide neither gold nor silver nor copper in your money belts, nor bag for your journey, nor two tunics, nor sandals, nor staffs; for a worker is worthy of his food. Now whatever city or town you enter, inquire who in it is worthy, and stay there till you go out. And when you go into a household, greet it. If the household is worthy, let your peace come upon it. But if it is not worthy, let your peace return to you. And whoever will not receive you nor hear your words, when you depart from that house or city, shake off the dust from your feet. Assuredly, I say to you, it will be more tolerable for the land of Sodom and Gomorrah in the day of judgment than for that city! Behold, I send you out as sheep in the midst of wolves. Therefore be wise as serpents and harmless as doves. But beware of men, for they will deliver you up to councils and scourge you in their synagogues. You will be brought before governors and kings for My sake, as a testimony to them and to the Gentiles. But when they deliver you up, do not worry about how or what you should speak. For it will be given to you in that hour what you should speak; for it is not you who speak, but the Spirit of your Father who speaks in you.

"Now brother will deliver up brother to death, and a father his child; and children will rise up against parents and cause them to be put to death. And you will be hated by all for My name's sake. But he who endures to the end will be saved. When they persecute you in this city, flee to another. For assuredly, I say to you, you will not have gone through the cities of Israel before the Son of Man comes. A disciple is not above his teacher, nor a servant above his master. It is enough for a disciple that he be like his teacher, and a servant like his master. If they have called the master of the house Beelzebub, how much more will they call those of his household! Therefore do not fear them. For there is nothing covered that will not be revealed, and hidden that will not be known. Whatever I tell you in the dark, speak in the light; and what you hear in the ear, preach on the housetops. And do not fear those who kill the body but cannot kill the soul. But rather fear Him who is able to destroy both soul and body in hell. Are not two sparrows sold for a copper coin? And not one of them falls to the ground apart from your Father's will. But the very hairs of your head are all numbered. Do not fear therefore; you are of more value than many sparrows. Therefore whoever confesses Me before men, him I will also confess before My Father who is in heaven. But whoever denies Me before men, him I will also deny before My Father who is in heaven. Do not think that I came to bring peace on earth. I did not come to bring peace but a sword. For I have come to 'set a man against his father, a daughter against her mother, and a daughter-in-law against her mother-in-law'; and 'a man's enemies will be those of his own household.' He who loves father or mother more than Me is not worthy of Me. And he who loves son or daughter more than Me is not worthy of Me. And he who does not take his cross and follow after Me is not worthy of Me. He who finds his life will lose it, and he who loses his life for My sake will find it. He who receives you receives Me, and he who receives Me receives Him who sent Me. He who receives a prophet in the name of a prophet shall receive a prophet's reward. And he who receives a righteous man in the name of a righteous man shall receive a righteous man's reward. And whoever gives one of these little ones only a cup of cold water in the name of a disciple, assuredly, I say to you, he shall by no means lose his reward." (Matthew 10:1–42)

Now it came to pass, when Jesus finished commanding His twelve disciples, that He departed from there to teach and to preach in their cities. And when John had heard in prison about the works of Christ, he sent two of his disciples and said to Him, "Are you the Coming One, or do we look for another?" Jesus answered and said to them, "Go and tell John the things which you hear and see: the blind see and the lame walk; the lepers are cleansed and the deaf hear; the dead are raised up and the poor have the gospel preached to them. And blessed is he who is not offended because of Me."

As they departed, Jesus began to say to the multitudes concerning John: "What did you go out into the wilderness to see? A reed shaken in the wind? But what did you go out to see? A man clothed in soft garments? Indeed, those who wear soft clothing are in kings' houses. But what did you go out to see? A prophet? Yes, I say to you, and more than a prophet. For this is he of whom it is written: 'Behold, I send My messenger before Your face, Who will prepare Your way before You.' Assuredly, I say to you, among those born of women there has not risen one greater than John the Baptist; but he who is least in the kingdom of heaven is greater than he. And from the days of John the Baptist until now the kingdom of heaven suffers violence, and the violent take it by force. For all the prophets and the law prophesied until John. And if you are willing to receive it, he is Elijah who is to come. He who has ears to hear, let him hear! But to what shall I liken this generation? It is like children sitting in the marketplaces and calling to their companions, and saying: 'We played the flute for you, And you did not dance; We mourned to you, And you did not lament.' For John came neither eating nor drinking, and they say, 'He has a demon.' The Son of Man came eating and drinking, and they say, 'Look, a glutton and a winebibber, a friend of tax collectors and sinners!' But wisdom is justified by her children."

Then He began to rebuke the cities in which most of His mighty works had been done, because they did not repent: "Woe to you, Chorazin! Woe to you, Bethsaida! For if the mighty works which were done in you had been done in Tyre and Sidon, they would have repented long ago in sackcloth and ashes. But I say to you, it will be more tolerable for Tyre and Sidon in the day of judgment than for you. And you, Capernaum, who are exalted to heaven, will be brought down to Hades; for if the mighty works which were done in you had been done in Sodom, it would have remained until this day. But I say to you that it shall be more tolerable for the land of Sodom in the day of judgment than for you" At that time Jesus answered and said, "I thank You, Father, Lord of heaven and earth, that You have hidden these things from the wise and prudent and have revealed them to babes. Even so, Father, for so it seemed good in Your sight. All things have been delivered to Me by My Father, and no one knows the Son except the Father. Nor does anyone know the Father except the Son, and the one to whom the Son wills to reveal Him. Come to Me, you who labor and are heavy laden, and I will give you rest. Take My yoke upon you and learn from Me, for I am gentle and lowly in heart, and you will find rest for your souls. For My yoke is easy and My burden is light." (Matthew 11:1–30)

At that time Jesus went through the grain fields on the Sabbath. And His disciples were hungry, and began to pluck heads of grain and to eat. And when the Pharisees saw it, they said to Him, "Look, Your disciples are doing what is not lawful to do on the Sabbath!" But He said to them, "Have you not read what David did when he was hungry, he and those who were with him: how he entered the house of God and ate the show bread which was not lawful for him to eat, nor for those who were with him, but only for the priests? Or have you not read in the law that on the Sabbath the priests in the temple profane the Sabbath, and are blameless? Yet I say to you that in this place there is One greater than the temple.

But if you had known what this means, 'I desire mercy and not sacrifice,' you would not have condemned the guiltless. For the Son of Man is Lord even of the Sabbath."

Now when He had departed from there, He went into their synagogue. And behold, there was a man who had a withered hand. And they asked Him, saying, "Is it lawful to heal on the Sabbath?"—that they might accuse Him. Then He said to them, "What man is there among you who has one sheep, and if it falls into a pit on the Sabbath, will not lay hold of it and lift it out? Of how much more value then is a man than a sheep? Therefore it is lawful to do good on the Sabbath." Then He said to the man, "Stretch out your hand." And he stretched it out, and it was restored as whole as the other. Then the Pharisees went out and plotted against Him, how they might destroy Him. But when Jesus knew it, He withdrew from there. And great multitudes followed Him, and He healed them all. Yet He warned them not to make Him known, that it might be fulfilled which was spoken by Isaiah the prophet, saying: "Behold! My Servant whom I have chosen, My Beloved in whom My soul is well pleased! I will put My Spirit upon Him, and He will declare justice to the Gentiles. He will not quarrel nor cry out, nor will anyone hear His voice in the streets. A bruised reed He will not break, And smoking flax He will not quench, till He sends forth justice to victory; And in His name Gentiles will trust."

Then one was brought to Him who was demon-possessed blind and mute; and He healed him, so that the blind and mute man both spoke and saw. And all the multitudes were amazed and said, "Could this be the Son of David?" But when the Pharisees heard, it they said, "This fellow does not cast out demons except by beelzebub, the ruler of the demons." But Jesus knew their thoughts, and said to them: "Every kingdom divided against itself is brought to desolation, and every city or house divided against itself will not stand. If satan cast out satan, he is divided against himself. How then will his kingdom stand? And if I cast out demons by beelzebub, by whom do your sons cast them out? Therefore, they shall be your judges. But if I cast out demons by the Spirit of God, surely the kingdom of God has come upon you. Or how can one enter a strong man's house and plunder his goods, unless he first binds the strong man? And then he will plunder his house. He who is not with Me is against Me, and he who does not gather with Me scatters abroad. Therefore, I say to you, every sin and blasphemy will be forgiven men, but the blasphemy against the Spirit will not be forgiven men. Anyone who speak a word against the Son of Man, it will be forgiven him; but whoever speaks against the Holy Spirit, it will not be forgiven him, either in this age or in the age to come. Either make the tree good and its fruit good, or else make the tree bad and its fruit bad; for a tree is known by its fruit. Brood of vipers! How can you, being evil speak good things? For out of the abundance of the heart the mouth speak. A good man out of the good treasure of his heart brings forth good things, and an evil man out of the evil treasure brings forth evil things. But I say to you that for every idle word men may speak, they will give account of it in the day of judgment. For by your words you will be justified, and by your words you will be condemned."

Then some of the scribes and Pharisees answered, saying, "Teacher, we want to see a sign from You." But He answered and said to them, "An evil and adulterous generation seeks after a sign, and no sign will be given to except the sign of the prophet Jonah. For as Jonah was three days and three nights in the belly of the great fish, so will the Son of Man be three days and nights in the heart of the earth. The men of Nineveh will rise up in the judgment with this generation and condemn it, because they repented at the preaching of Jonah; and indeed a greater than Jonah is here. The queen of the south will rise up in the judgment with this generation and condemn it, for she came from the ends of the earth to hear the wisdom of Solomon; and indeed a greater than Solomon is here. When an unclean spirit goes out of a man, he goes through dry places, seeking rest, and finds none. Then he says, 'I will return to my house from which I came.' And when he comes, he finds it empty, swept, and put in order. Then he goes and takes with him seven other spirits more wicked than himself, and they enter and dwell there; and the last state of that man is worse than the first. So shall it also be with this wicked generation."

While He was still talking to the multitudes, behold, His mother and brothers stood outside, seeking to speak with Him. Then one said to Him, "Look, Your mother and Your brothers are standing outside, seeking to speak with You." But He answered and said to the one who told Him, "Who is My mother and who are My brothers?" And He stretched out His hand toward His disciples and said, "Here are My mother and My brothers! For whoever does the will of My Father in heaven is My brother and sister and mother." (Matthew 12:1–50)

On the same day Jesus went out of the house and sat by the sea. And great multitudes were gathered together to Him, so that He got into a boat and sat; and the whole multitude stood on the shore. Then He spoke many things to them in parables, saying: "Behold, a sower went out to sow. And as he sowed, some seed fell by the wayside; and the birds came and devoured them. Some fell on stony places, where they did not have much earth; and they immediately sprang up because they had no depth of earth. But when the sun was up they were scorched, and because they had no root they withered away. And some fell among thorns, and the thorns sprang up and choked them But others fell on good ground and yielded a crop: some a hundredfold, some sixty, some thirty. He who has ears to hear, let him hear!"

And the disciples came and said to Him, "Why do You speak to them in parables?" He answered and said to them, "Because it has been given to you to know the mysteries of the kingdom of heaven, but to them it has not been given. For whoever has, to him more will be given, and he will have abundance; but whoever does not have, even what he has will be taken away from him. Therefore, I speak to them in parables, because seeing they do not see, and hearing they do not hear, nor do they understand. And in them the prophecy of Isaiah is fulfilled, which says: 'Hearing you will hear and shall not understand,

And seeing you will see and not perceive; for the hearts of this people have grown dull. Their ears are hard of hearing, And their eyes they have closed, lest they should see with their eyes and hear with their ears, lest they should understand with their hearts and turn, so that I should heal them.' But blessed are your eyes for they see, and your ears for they hear; for assuredly, I say to you that many prophets and righteous men desired to see what you see, and did not see it, and to hear what you hear, and did not hear it. Therefore, hear the parable of the sower: when anymore hears the word of the kingdom, and does not understand it, then the wicked one comes and snatches away what was sown in his heart. This is he who received seed by the wayside. But he who received the seed on stony places, this is he who hears the word and immediately receives it with joy; yet he has no root in himself, but endures only for a while. For when tribulation or persecution arises because of the word, immediately he stumbles. Now he received seed among the thorns is he who hears the word, and the cares of this world and the deceitfulness of riches choke the word, and he becomes unfruitful. But he who received seed on the good ground is he who hears the word and understands it, who indeed bears fruit and produces: some a hundredfold, some sixty, some thirty."

Another parable He put forth to them, saying: "The kingdom of heaven is like a man who sowed good seed in his field; but while men slept, his enemy came and sowed tares among the wheat and went his way. But when the grain had sprouted and produced a crop, then the tares also appeared. So the servants of the owner came and said to him, 'Sir, did you not sow good seeding your field? How then does it have tares?' He said to them, 'An enemy has done this.' The servants said to him, 'Do you want us then to go and gather them up?' But he said, 'No, lest while you gather up the tares you also uproot the wheat with them. Let both grow together until the harvest, and at the time of harvest I will say to the reapers, First, gather together the tares and bind them in bundles to burn them, but gather the wheat into my barn.'"

Another parable He put forth to them, saying: "The kingdom of heaven is like a mustard seed, which a man took and sowed in his field, which indeed is the least of all the seeds; but when it is grown it is greater than the herbs and becomes a tree, so that the birds of the air come and nest in its branches." Another parable He spoke to them: "The kingdom of heaven is like leaven, which a woman took and hid in three measures of meal till it was all leavened." All these things Jesus spoke to the multitude in parables; and without a parable He did not speak to them, that it might be fulfilled which was spoken by the prophet, saying: "I will open My mouth in parables; I will utter things kept secret from the foundation of the world." Then Jesus sent the multitude away and went into the house. And His disciples came to Him, saying, "Explain to us the parable of the tares of the field." He answered and said to them: "He who sows the good seed is the Son of Man. The field is world, the good seeds are the sons of the kingdom, but the tares are the sons of the wicked one. The enemy who sowed them is the devil, the harvest is the end of the age, and the reapers are the angels. Therefore, as the tares are gathered and burned in the fire, so it will be at the end of the age. The Son of Man will send out His angels, and they will gather out of His kingdom all things that offend, and those who practice lawlessness, and will cast them into the furnace of fire. There will be wailing and gnashing of teeth. Then the righteous will shine forth as the sun in the kingdom of their Father. He who has ears to hear, let him hear! Again, the kingdom of heaven is like treasure hidden in a field, which a man found and hid; and for joy over it he goes and sells all that he has and buys that field. Again, the kingdom of heaven is like a merchant seeking beautiful pearls, who, when he had found one pearl of great price, went and sold all that he had and bought it. Again, the kingdom of heaven is like a dragnet that was cast into the sea and gathered some of every kind, which, when it was full, they drew to shore; and they sat down and gathered the good into vessels, but threw the bad away. So it will be at the end of the age, the angels will come forth, separate the wicked from among the just, and cast them into the furnace of fire. There will be wailing and gnashing of teeth."

Jesus said to them, "Have you understood all these things?" They said to Him, "Yes, Lord." Then He said to them, "Therefore every scribe instructed concerning the kingdom of heaven is like a householder who brings out of his treasure things new and old." Now it came to pass, when Jesus had finished these parables, that He departed from there. Where He had come to His own country, He taught them in their synagogue, so that they were astonished and said, "Where did this Man get this wisdom and these mighty works? Is this not the carpenter's son? Is not His mother called Mary? And His brothers James, Joses, Simon, and Judes? And His sisters, are they not all with us? Where then did this Man get all these things?" So they were offended at Him. But Jesus said to them, "A prophet is not without honor except in his own country and in his own house." Now He did not do many mighty works there because of their unbelief. (Matthew 13:1–58)

At that time Herod, the tetrarch, heard the report about Jesus and said to his servants, "This is John the Baptist; he is risen from the dead, and therefore these powers are at work in him." For Herod had laid hold of John and bound him, and put him in prison for the sake of Herodias, his brother Philip's wife. Because John had sad to him, "It is not lawful for you to have her." And although he wanted to put him to death, he feared the multitude, because they counted him as a prophet. But when Herod's birthday was celebrated, the daughter of Herodias danced before them and pleased Herod. Therefore, he promised with an oath to give her whatever she might ask. So she, having been prompted by her mother, said, "Give me John the Baptist's head here on a platter." And the king was sorry; nevertheless, because of the oaths and because of those who sat with him, he commanded it to be given to her. So he sent and had John beheaded in prison. And his head was brought on a platter and given to the girl, and she brought it to her mother. Then his disciples came and took away the body and buried it, and went and told Jesus.

When Jesus heard it, He departed from there by boat to a deserted place by Himself. But when the multitudes heard it, they followed Him on foot from the cities. And when Jesus went out He saw a great multitude; and He was moved with compassion of them and healed their sick. When it was evening, His disciples came to Him, saying, "Tis is a deserted place, and the hour is already late. Send the multitudes away, that they may go into the villages and buy themselves food." But Jesus said to them, "They do not need to go away. You give them something to eat." And they said to Him, "Where have here only five loaves and two fish." He said, "Bring them here to Me." Then He commanded the multitudes to sit down on the grass. And He took the five loaves and the two fish, and looking up to heaven, He blessed and broke and gave the loaves to the disciples; and the disciples gave to multitudes. So they all ate and were filled, and they took up twelve baskets full of the fragments that remained. Now those who had eaten were about five thousand men, besides woman and children.

Immediately, Jesus made His disciples get into the boat and go before Him to the other side, while He sent the multitudes away. And when He had sent the multitudes away, He went up on the mountain by Himself to pray. Now when evening came, He was alone there. But the boat was now in the middle of the sea, tossed by the waves, for the wind was contrary. Now in the fourth watch of the night Jesus went to them, walking on the sea. And when the disciples saw Him walking on the sea, they were troubled, saying, "It is a ghost!" And they cried out for fear. But immediately, Jesus spoke to them,

## JESUS IS GOD

saying, "Be of good cheer! It is I do not be afraid." And Peter answered Him and said, "Lord, if it is You, command me to come to You on the water." So He said, "Come." And when Peter had come down out of the boat, he walked on the water to go to Jesus, but when he saw that the wind was boisterous, he was afraid; and beginning to sink he cried out, saying, "Lord, save me!

And immediately Jesus stretched out His hand and caught him, and said to him, "O you of little faith, why did you doubt?" And when they got into the boat, the wind ceased. Then those who were in the boat came and worshiped Him, saying, "Truly You are the Son of God."

When they had crossed over, they came to the land of Gennesaret. And when the men of that place recognized Him, they sent out into all that surrounding region, brought to Him all who were sick, and begged Him that they might only touch the hem of His garment. And as many as touched it were made perfectly well. (Matthew 14:1–36)

Then the scribes and Pharisees who were from Jerusalem came to Jesus, saying, "Why do You disciples transgress the tradition of the elders? For they do not wash their hands when they eat bread." He answered and said to them, "Why do you also transgress the commandment of God because of your traditions? For God command, saying, 'Honor your father and your mother' and 'He who Curses father or mother, let him be put to death.' But you say, 'Whoever says to his father or mother, "Whatever profit you might have received from me is a gift to God" then he need not honor his father or mother.' Thus, you have made the commandment of God of no effect by your tradition. Hypocrites! Well did Isaiah prophesy about you, saying: 'These people draw near to Me with their mouth, And honor Me with their lips, But their heart is far from Me. And in vain they worship Me, Teaching as doctrines the commandments men.'"

When He had called the multitude to Himself, He said to them, "Hear and understand: Not what goes into the mouth defiles a man; but what comes out of the mouth, this defiles a man." Then His disciples came and said to Him, "Do You know that the Pharisees were offended when they heard this saying?" But He answered and said, "Every plant which My heavenly Father has not planted will be uprooted. Let them alone. They are blind leader of the blind, and if the blind leads the blind, both will fall into a ditch." Then Peter answered and said to Him, "Explain this parable to us." So Jesus said, "Are you also still without understanding? Do you not yet understand that whatever enters the mouth goes into the stomach and is eliminated? But those things which proceed out of the mouth come from the heart, and they defile a man. For out of the heart proceed evil thoughts, murders, adulteries, fornications, thefts, false witness, blasphemies. These are the things which defile a man, but to eat with unwashed hands does not defile a man."

Then Jesus went out from there and departed to the region of Tyre and Sidon. And behold, a woman of Canaan came from that region and cried out to Him, saying, "Have mercy on me, O Lord, Son of David! My daughter is severely demon-possessed." But He answered her not a word. And His disciples came and urged Him, saying, "Send her away, for she cries out after us." But He answered and said, "I was not sent except to the lost sheep of the house of Israel." Then she came and worshiped Him, saying, "Lord, help me!" But He answered and said, "It is not good to take the children's bread and throw it to the little dogs." And she said, "Yes, Lord, yet even the little dogs eat the crumbs which falls from the master's table." Then Jesus answered and said to her daughter was healed from that very hour.

Jesus departed from there, skirted the Sea of Galilee and went up on the mountain and sat down there. Then great multitudes came to Him, having with them the lame, blind, mute, maimed, and many others; and they laid them down at Jesus' feet, and He healed them. So the multitude marveled when they saw the mute speaking, the maimed made whole, the lame walking, and the blind seeing; and they glorified the God of Israel.

Now Jesus called His disciples to Himself and said, "I have compassion on the multitude, because they have now continued with Me three days and have nothing to eat. And I do not want to send them away hungry, lest they faint on the way." Then His disciples said to Him, "Where could we get enough bread in the wilderness to fill such a great multitude?" Jesus said to them, "How many loaves do you have?" And they said, "Seven, and a few little fish." So He commanded the multitude to sit down on the ground. And He took the seven loaves and the fish and gave thanks, broke them and gave them to His disciples; and the disciples gave to the multitude. So they all ate and were filled, and they took up seven large baskets full of the fragments that were left. Now those who ate were four thousand men, besides woman and children. And He sent away the multitude, got into the boat, and came to the region of Mandala. (Matthew 15:1–39)

Then the Pharisees and Sadducees came, and testing Him asked that He would show them a sign from heaven. He answered and said to them, "When it is evening you say, 'It will be fair weather, for the sky is red'; and in the morning, 'It will be foul weather today, for the sky is red and threatening.' Hypocrites! You know how to discern the face of the sky, but you cannot discern the signs of the times. A wicked and adulterous generation seeks after a sign, and no sign shall be given to it except the sign of the prophet Jonah."

And He left them and departed. Now when His disciples had come to the other side, they had forgotten to take bread. Then Jesus said to them, "Take heed and beware of the leaven of the Pharisees and the Sadducees." And they reasoned among themselves, saying, "It is because we have taken no bread." But Jesus, being aware of it, said to them, "You of little faith, why do you reason among yourselves because you have brought no bread? Do you not yet understand, or remember the five loaves of the five thousand and how many baskets you took up? Nor the seven loaves of the four thousand and how many large baskets you took up? How is it you do not understand that I did not speak to you concerning bread?—but to beware of the leaven of the Pharisees and Sadducees." Then they understood that He did not tell them to beware of the leaven of bread, but of the doctrine of the Pharisees and Sadducees.

## JESUS IS GOD

When Jesus came into the region of Caesarea Philippi, He asked His disciples, saying, "Who do men say that I, the Son of Man, am?" So they said, "Some say John the Baptist, some Elijah, and others Jeremiah or one of the prophets." He said to them, "But who do you say that I am?" Simon Peter answered and said, "You are the Christ, the Son of the living God." Jesus answered and said to him, "Blessed are you, Simon Bar-Jonah, for flesh and blood has not revealed this to you, but My Father who is in heaven. And I also say to you that you are Peter, and on this rock I will build My church, and the gates of Hades shall not prevail against it. And I will give you the keys of the kingdom of heaven, and whatever you bind on earth will be bound in heaven, and whatever you loose on earth will be loosed in heaven." Then He commanded His disciples that they should tell no one that He was Jesus the Christ. From that time Jesus began to show to His disciples that He must go to Jerusalem, and suffer many things from the elders and chief priests and scribes, and be killed, and be raised the third day. Then Peter took Him aside and began to rebuke Him, saying, "Far be it from You, Lord; this shall not happen to You!" But He turned and said to Peter, "Get behind Me, satan! You are an offense to Me, for you are not mindful of the things of God, but the things of men." Then Jesus said to His disciples, "If anyone desires to come after Me, let him deny himself, and take up his cross, and follow Me. For whoever desires to save his life will lose it, but whoever loses his life for My sake will find it. For what profit is it to a man if he gains the whole world, and loses his own soul? For the Son of Man will come in the glory of His

Father with His angels, and then He will reward each according to his works. Assuredly, I say to you, there are some standing here who shall not taste death till they see the Son of Man coming in His kingdom." (Matthew 16:1–28)

Now after six days Jesus took Peter, James, and John his brother, led them up on a high mountain by themselves; and He was transfigured before them. His face shone like the sun, and His clothes became as white as the light. And behold, Moses and Elijah appeared to them, talking with Him. Then Peter answered and said to Jesus, "Lord, it is good for us to be here; if You wish, let us make here three tabernacles: one for You, one for Moses, and one for Elijah."

While he was still speaking, behold, a bright cloud overshadowed them; and suddenly a voice came out of the cloud, saying, "This is My beloved Son, in whom I am well pleased. Hear Him!" And when the disciples heard it, they fell on their faces and were greatly afraid. But Jesus came and touched them and said, "Arise, and do not be afraid." When they had lifted up their eyes, they saw no one but Jesus only. Now as they came down from the mountain, Jesus commanded them, saying, "Tell the vision to no one until the Son of Man is risen from the dead." And His disciples asked Him, saying, "Why then do the scribes say that Elijah must come first?" Jesus answered and said to them, "Indeed, Elijah is coming first and will restore all things. But I say to you that Elijah has come already, and they did not know him but did to him whatever they wished. Likewise, the Son of Man is also about to

# JESUS IS GOD

suffer at their hands." Then the disciples understood that He spoke to them of John the Baptist.

And when they had come to the multitude, a man came to Him, kneeling down to Him and saying, "Lord, have mercy on my son, for he is an epileptic and suffers severely; for he often falls into the fire and often into the water. So I brought him to Your disciples, but they could not cure him." Then Jesus answered and said, "O fatherless and perverse generation, how long shall I be with you? How long shall I bear with you? Bring him here to Me." And Jesus rebuked the demon, and it came out of him; and the child was cured from that very hour. Then the disciples came to Jesus privately and said, "Why could we not cast it out?" So Jesus said to them, "Because of your unbelief; for assuredly, I say to you, if you have faith as a mustard seed, you will say to this mountain, move; and nothing will be impossible for you. However, this kind does not go out except by prayer and fasting."

Now while they were staying in Galilee, Jesus said to them, "The Son of Man is about to be betrayed into the hands of men, and they will kill Him, and the third day He will be raised up." And they were exceedingly sorrowful. When they had come to Capernaum, those who received the temple tax came to Peter and said, "Does your Teacher not pay the temple tax?" He said, "Yes." And when he had come into the house, Jesus anticipated him, saying, "What do you think, Simon? From whom do the kings of the earth take customs or taxes, from their sons or from strangers?" Peter said to Him, "From strangers." Jesus said to him, "Then the sons are free. Nevertheless, lest we offend them, go to the sea, cast in a hook, and take the fish that comes up first. And when you have opened its mouth, you will find a piece of money; take that and give it to them for Me and you." (Matthew 17:1–27)

At that time the disciples came to Jesus, saying, "Who then is greatest in the kingdom of heaven?" Then Jesus called a little child to Him, set him in the midst of them, and said, "Assuredly, I say to you, unless you are converted and become as little children, you will by no means enter the kingdom of heaven. Therefore, whoever humbles himself as this little child is the greatest in the kingdom of heaven. Whoever receives one little child like this in My name receives Me. But whoever causes one of these little ones who believe in Me to sin, it would be better for him if a millstone were hung around his neck, and he were drowned in the depths the sea. Woe to the world because of offenses! For offenses must come, but woe to that man by whom the offense comes! If your hand or foot cause you to sin, cut it off and cast it from you. It is better for you to enter into life lame or maimed, rather than having two hands or two feet, to be cast into the everlasting fire. And if your eye causes you to sin, pluck it out and cast it from you. It is better for you to enter into life with one eye, rather than having two eyes, to be cast into hell fire. Take heed that you do not despise one of these little ones, for I say to you that in heaven their angels always see the face of My Father who is in heaven. For the Son of Man has come to save that which was lost. What do you think? If a man has a hundred sheep, and one of them goes astray, does he not leave the ninety-nine and go to the mountains to seek the one that is straying? And if he should find it, assuredly, I say to you, he rejoices more over that sheep than over the ninety-nine that did not go astray. Even so it is not the will of your Father who is in heaven that one of these little ones should perish. Moreover, if your brother sins against you, go and tell him his fault between you and him alone. If he hears you, you have gained your brother. But if he will not hear, take with you one or two more, that 'by the mouth of two or three witnesses every word may be established.' And if he refuses to hear them tell it to the church. But if he refuses even to hear the church, let him be to you like a heathen and a tax collector. Assuredly, I say to you, whatever you bind on earth will be bound in heaven, and whatever you loose on earth will be loosed in heaven. Again I say to you that if two of you agree on earth concerning anything that they ask, it will be done for them by My Father in heaven. For where two or three are gathered together in My name, I am there in the midst of them."

Then Peter came to Him and said, "Lord, how often shall my brother sin against me, and I forgive him? Up to seven times?" Jesus said to him, "I do not say to you, up to seven times, but up to seventy times seven. Therefore, the kingdom of heaven is like a certain king who wanted to settle accounts with his servants. And when he had begun to settle accounts, one was brought to him who owed him ten thousand talents. But as he was not able to pay, his master commanded that he be sold, with his wife and children and all that he had, and that payment be made. The servant therefore fell down before him, saying, 'Master, have patience with me, and I will pay you all.' Then the master of that servant was moved with compassion, released him, and forgave him the debt. But that servant went out and found one of his fellow servants who owed him a hundred denarii; and he laid hands on him and took him by the throat, saying, 'Pay me what you owe!' So his fellow servant fell down at his feet and begged him, saying, 'Have patience with me, and I will pay you all.' And he would not, but went and threw him into prison till he should pay the debt. So when his fellow servants saw what had been done, they were very grieved, and came and told their master all that had been done. Then his master, after he had called him, said to him, 'You wicked servant! I forgave you all that debt because you begged me. Should you not also have had compassion on your fellow servant, just as I had pity on you?' And his master was angry, and delivered him to the torturers until he should pay all that was due to him. So My heavenly Father also will do to you if each of you, from his heart, does not forgive his brother his trespasses." (Matthew 18:1–35)

Now it came to pass, when Jesus had finished these sayings, that He departed from Galilee and came to the region of Judea beyond the Jordan. And great multitudes followed Him, and He healed them there. The Pharisees also came to Him, testing Him, and saying to Him, "Is it lawful for a man to divorce his wife for just any reason?" And He answered and said to them, "Have you not read that He who made them at the Beginning made them male and female and said, 'For this reason a man shall leave his father and mother and be join to his wife, and the two shall become one flesh'? So then they are no longer two but one flesh. Therefore, what God has joined together, let not man separate." They said to Him, "Why then did Moses command to give a certificate of divorce, and to put her away?" He said to them, "Moses, because of the hardness of your hearts, permitted you to divorce your wives, but from the beginning it was not so. And I say to you, whoever divorces his wife, except for sexual immorality, and marries another, commits adultery; and whoever marries her who is divorced commits adultery." His disciples said to Him, "If such is the case of the man with his wife, it is better not to Mary." But He said to them, "All cannot accept this saying, but only those to whom it has been given: for there are eunuchs who were born thus from their mother's womb, and there are eunuchs who were made eunuchs by men, and there are eunuchs who have made themselves eunuchs for the kingdom of heaven's sake. He who is able to accept it, let him accept it."

Then little children were brought to Him that He might put His hands on them and pray, but the disciples rebuked them. But Jesus said, "Let the little children come to Me, and do not forbid them; for of such is the kingdom of heaven." And He laid His hands on them and departed from there. Now behold, one came and said to Him, "Good Teacher, what good thing shall I do that I may have eternal life?" So He said to him, "Why do you call Me good? No one is good but One, that is, God. But if you want to enter into life, keep the commandments." He said to Him, "Which ones?" Jesus said, "'You shall not murder,' 'You shall not commit adultery,' 'You shall not steal,' 'You shall not bear false witness,' 'Honor your father and your mother,' and 'You shall love your neighbor as yourself.'" The young man said to Him, "All these things I have kept from my youth. What do I still lack?" Jesus said to him, "If you want to be perfect, go sell what you have and give to the poor, and you will have treasure in heaven; and come, follow Me." But when the young man heard that saying, he went away sorrowful, for he had great possessions. Then Jesus said to His disciples, "Assuredly, I say to you that it is hard for a rich man to enter the kingdom of heaven. And again I say to you, it is easier for a camel to go through the eye of a needle than for a rich man to enter the kingdom of God." When His disciples heard it, they were greatly astonished, saying, "Who then can be saved?" But Jesus looked at them and said to them, "With men this is impossible, but with God all things are possible." Then Peter answered and said to Him, "See, we have left all and followed You. Therefore what shall we have?" So Jesus said to them, "Assuredly I say to you, that in the regeneration, when the Son of Man sits on the throne of His glory, you who have followed Me will also sit on twelve thrones, judging the twelve tribes of Israel. And everyone who has left houses of brothers or sisters of father or mother or wife or children or lands, for My name's sake, shall receive a hundredfold, and inherit eternal life. But many who are first will be last, and the last first. (Matthew 19:1–30)

"For the kingdom of heaven is like a landowner who went out early in the morning to hire laborers for his vineyard. Now when he had agreed with the laborers for a denarius a day. He sent them into his vineyard. And he went out about the third hour and saw others standing idle in the marketplace, and said to them, 'You also go into the vineyard, and whatever is right I will give you.' So they went. Again he went out about the sixth and the ninth hour, and did likewise. And about the eleventh hour he went out and found others standing idle, and said to them, 'Why have you been standing here idle all day?' They said to him, 'Because no one hired us.' He said to them, 'You also go into the vineyard, and whatever is right you will receive.' So when evening had come, the owner of the vineyard said to his steward, 'Call the laborers and give them their wages, beginning with the last to the first.' And when those came who were hired about the eleventh hour, they each received a denarius. But when the first came, they supposed that they would receive more; and they likewise received each a denarius. And when they had received it, they complained against the landowner, saying, 'These last men have worked only one hour, and you made them equal to us who have borne the burden and heat of the day.' But he answered one of them and said, 'Friend, I am doing you no wrong. Did you not agree with me for a denarius? Take what is your and go your way. I wish to give to this last man the same as to you. Is it not lawful for me to do what I wish with my own things? Or is your eye evil because I am good?' So the last will be first, and the first last. For many are called, but few chosen."

Now Jesus, going up to Jerusalem, took the twelve disciples aside on the road and said to them, "Behold, we are going up to Jerusalem, and the Son of Man will be betrayed to the chief priest and to the scribes; and they with condemn Him to death, and deliver Him to the Gentiles to mock and scourge and to crucify. And the third day He will rise again." Then the mother of Zebedee's sons came to Him with her sons, kneeling down and asking something from Him. And He said to her, "What do you wish?" She said to Him, "Grant that these two sons of mine may sit, one on Your right hand and the other on the left, in Your kingdom." But Jesus answered and said, "You do not know what you ask. Are you able to drink the cup that I am about to drink, and be baptized with the baptism that I am baptized with?" They said to Him, "We are able." So He said to them, "You will indeed drink My cup, and be baptized with the baptism that I am baptized with; but to sit on My right hand and on My left is not Mine to give, but it is for those for whom it is prepared by My Father." And when the ten heard it, they were greatly displeased with the two brothers. But Jesus called them to Himself and said, "You know that the rulers of the Gentiles lord it over them, and those who are great exercise authority over them. Yet it shall not be so among you; but whatever desires to become great among you, let him be your servant. And whoever desires to be first among you, let him be your slave—Just as the Son of Man did not come to be served, but to serve, and to give His life a ransom for many."

Now as they went out of Jericho, a great multitude followed Him. And behold, two blind men sitting by the road, when they heard that Jesus was passing by, cried out, saying, "Have mercy on us Lord, Son of David!" Then the multitude warned them that they should be quiet;

## JESUS IS GOD

but they cried out all the more, saying, "Have mercy on us, O Lord, Son of David!" So Jesus stood still and called them, and said, "What do you want Me to do for you?" They said to Him, "Lord, that our eyes may be opened." So Jesus had compassion and touched their eyes. And immediately their eyes received sight, and they followed Him. (Matthew 20:1–34)

Now when they drew near Jerusalem, and came to Bethphage, at the Mount of Olives, then Jesus sent two disciples, saying to them, "Go into the village opposite you, and immediately you will find a donkey tied, and a colt with her. Loose them and bring them to Me. And if anyone says anything to you, you shall say, 'The Lord has need of them,' and immediately he will send them." All this was done that it might be fulfilled which was spoken by the prophet, saying: "Tell the daughter of Zion, 'Behold, your King is coming to you, Lowly, and sitting on a donkey, A colt, the foal of a donkey.'" So the disciples went and did as Jesus commanded them. They brought the donkey and the colt, laid their clothes on them, and set Him on them. And a very great multitude speed their clothes on the road; others cut down branches from the trees and spread them on the road. Then the multitudes who went before and those who followed cried out, saying: "Hosanna to the Son of David! 'Blessed is He who comes in the name of the Lord!' Hosanna in the highest!" And when He had come into Jerusalem, all the city was moved, saying, "Who is this?" So the multitudes said, "This is Jesus, the prophet from Nazareth of Galilee." Then Jesus went into the temple of God and drove out all those who bought and sold in the temple, and overturned the tables of the money changers and the seats of those who sold doves. And He said to them, "It is written, 'My house shall be called a house of prayer,' but you have made it a den of thieves." Then the blind and the lame came to Him in the temple, and He healed them. But when the chief priests and scribes saw the wonderful things that He did and the children crying out in the temple and saying, "Hosanna to the Son of David!" they were indignant and said to Him, "Do You hear what these are say?" And Jesus said to them, "Yes. Have you never read, 'Out of the mouth of babes and nursing infants You have perfected praise'?"

Then He left them and went out of the city to Bethany, and He lodged there. Now in the morning, as He returned to the city, He was hungry. And seeing a fig tree by the road, He came to it and found nothing on it but leaves, and said to it, "Let no fruit grow on you ever again." Immediately, the fig tree withered away. And when the disciples saw it, they marveled, saying, "How did the fig tree wither away so soon?" So Jesus answered and said to them, "Assuredly, I say to you, if you have faith and do not doubt, you will not only do what was done to the fig tree, but also if you say to this mountain, 'Be removed and be cast into the sea,' it will be done. And whatever things you ask in prayer, believing, you will receive."

Now when He came into the temple, the chief priests and the elders of the people confronted Him as He was teaching, and said, "By what authority are You doing these things? And who gave You this authority?" But Jesus answered and said to them, "I also will ask you one thing,

JESUS IS GOD

which if you tell Me, I likewise will tell you by what authority I do these things: The baptism of John—where was it from? From heaven or from men?" And they reasoned among themselves, saying, "If we say, 'From heaven,' He will say to us, 'Why then did you not believe him?' But if we say, 'From men,' we fear the multitude, for all count John as a prophet." So they answered Jesus and said, "We do not know." And He said to them, "Neither will I tell you by what authority I do these things. But what do you think? A man had two sons, and he came to the first and said, 'Son, go, work today in my vineyard.' He answered and said, 'I will not,' but afterward he regretted it and went. Then he came to the second and said likewise. And he answered and said, 'I go, sir,' but he did not go. Which of the two did the will of his father?" They said to Him, "The first." Jesus said to them, "As surely, I say to you that tax collectors and harlots enter the kingdom of God before you. For John came to you in the way of righteousness, and you did not believe him; but tax collectors and harlots believed him; and when you saw it, you did not afterward relent and believe him. Hear another parable: there was a certain landowner who planted a vineyard and set a hedge around it, dug a winepress in it and built a tower. And he leased it to vinedressers and went into a far country. Now when vintage-time drew near, he sent his servants to the vinedressers, that they might receive its fruit. And the vinedressers took his servants, beat one, killed one, and stoned another. Again he sent other servants, more than the first, and they did likewise to them. Then last of all he sent his son to them, saying, 'They will respect my son.'

But when the vinedressers saw the son, they said among themselves, 'This is the heir. Come, let us kill him and seize his inheritance.' So they took him and cast him out of the vineyard and killed him. Therefore, when the owner of the vineyard comes, what will he do to those vinedressers?" They said to Him, "He will destroy those wicked men miserably, and lease his vineyard to other vinedressers who will render to him the fruits in their seasons." Jesus said to them, "Have you never read in the Scriptures: 'The stones which the builders rejected has become the chief cornerstone. This was the LORD's doing, and it is marvelous in our eyes'? Therefore I say to you, the kingdom of God will be taken from you and given to a nation bearing the fruits of it. And whoever falls on this stone will be broken; but on whomever it falls, it will grind him to powder." Now when the chief priests and Pharisees heard His parables, they perceived that He was speaking of them. But when they sought to lay hands on Him, they feared the multitudes, because they took Him for a prophet. (Matthew 21:1–46)

And Jesus answered and spoke to them again by parables and said: "The kingdom of heaven is like a certain king who arranged a marriage for his son, and sent out his servants to call those who were invited to the wedding; and they were not willing to come. again he sent out other servants, saying, 'Tell those who are invited, "See, I have prepared my dinner; my oxen and fatted cattle are killed, and all things are ready. Come to the wedding."' But they made light of it and went their ways, one to his own farm, another to his business. And the rest seized his servants, treated them spitefully, and killed them. But when the king heard about it, he was furious. And he sent out his armies, destroyed those murderers, and burned up their city. Then he said to his servants, 'The wedding is ready, but those who were invited were not worthy. Therefore, go into the highways, and as many as you find, invite to wedding.' So those servants went out into the highways and gathered together all whom they found, both bad and good. And the wedding hall was filled with guests. But when the king came in to see the guests, he saw a man there who did not have on a wedding garment. So he said to him, 'Friend, how did you come in here without a wedding garment?' And he was speechless. Then the king said to the servants, 'Bind him hand and foot, take him away, and cast him into outer darkness; there will be weeping and gnashing of teeth.' For many are called, but few are chosen."

Then the Pharisees went and plotted how they might entangle Him in His talk. And they sent to Him their disciples with the Herodians, saying, "Teacher, we know that You are true, and teach the way of God in truth; nor do You care about anyone, for You do not regard the person of men. Tell us, therefore, what do You think? Is it lawful to pay taxes to Caesar, or not?" But Jesus perceived their wickedness and said, "Why do you test Me, you hypocrites? Show Me the tax money." So they brought Him a denarius. And He said to them, "Whose image and inscription is this?" They said to Him, "Caesar's." And He said to them, "Render therefore to Caesar the things that are Caesar's and to God the things that are God's." When they had heard these words, they marveled, and left Him and went their way.

The same day the Sadducees, who say there is no resurrection, came to Him and asked Him, saying: "Teacher, Moses said that if a man dies, having no children, his brother shall marry his wife and raise up offspring for his brother. Now there were with us seven brother. The first died after he had married, and having no offspring, left his wife to his brother. Likewise the second also, and the third, even to the seventh. Last of all the woman died also. Therefore, in the resurrection, whose wife of the seven will she be? For they all had her." Jesus answered and said to them, "You are mistaken, not knowing the Scriptures nor the power of God. For in the resurrection they neither marry nor are given in marriage, but are like angels of God in heaven. But concerning the resurrection of the dead, have you not read what was spoken to you by God, saying, 'I am the God of Abraham, the God of Isaac, and the God of Jacob'? God is not the God of the dead, but of the living." And when the multitudes heard this, they were astonished at His teaching. But when the Pharisees heard that He had silenced the Sadducees, they gathered together. Then one of them, a lawyer, asked Him a question, testing Him, and saying, "Teacher, which is the great commandment in the law?" Jesus said to him, "'You shall love the Lord your God with all your heart, with all your soul, and with all your mind.' This is the first and great commandment. And the second is like it: 'You shall love your neighbor as yourself.' On these two commandments hang all the Law and the Prophets." While the Pharisees were gathered together, Jesus asked them, saying, "What do you think about the Christ? Whose Son is He?" They said to Him,

## JESUS IS GOD

"The Son of David." He said to them, "How then does David in the Spirit call Him Lord saying: 'The Lord said, "My Lord, sit at My right hand, till I make Your enemies Your footstool"'? If David then calls Him 'Lord,' how is He his Son?" And no one was able to answer Him a word, nor from that day on did anyone dare question Him anymore. (Matthew 22:1–46)

Then Jesus spoke to the multitude and to His disciples, saying: "There scribes and the Pharisees sit in Moses' seat. Therefore, whatever they tell you to observe, that observe and do, but do not do according to their works; for they say, and do not do. For they bind heavy burdens, hard to bear, and lay them on men's shoulders; but they themselves will not move them with one of their fingers. But all their works they do to be seen by men. They make their phylacteries broad and enlarge the borders of their garments. They love the best place in the feast, the best seats in the synagogues, greetings in the marketplaces, and to be called by men, 'Rabbi, Rabbi.' But you, do not be called 'Rabbi'; for One is your Teacher, the Christ, and you are all brethren. Do not call anyone on earth your father; for One is your Father, He who is in heaven. And do not be called teachers; for One is your Teacher, the Christ. But he who is greatest among you shall be your servant. And who ever exalts himself will be humbled, and he who humbles himself will be exalted. But woe to you, scribes and Pharisees, hypocrites! For you shut up the kingdom of heaven against men; for you neither go in yourselves, nor do you allow those who are entering to go in. Woe to you, scribes and Pharisees, hypocrites! For you devour widows' houses, and for a pretense make long prayers. Therefore, you will receive greater condemnation. Woe to you, scribes and Pharisees, hypocrites! For you travel land and to win on proselyte, and when he is won, you make him twice as much a son of hell as yourselves. Woe to you, blind guides, who say, 'Whoever swear by the temple, it is nothing; but whoever swears by the gold of the temple, he is obliged to perform it.' Fools and blind! For which is greater, the gold or the temple that sanctifies the gold? And 'Whoever swears by the altar, it is nothing; but whoever swears by the gift that is on it, he is obliged to perform it.' Fools and blind! For which is greater, the gift or the alter that sanctifies the gift? Therefore, he who swears by the altar, swears by it by all things it. He who swears by the temple, swears by it and by Him who dwells in it. And he who swears by heaven, swears by the throne of God and by Him who sits on it. Woe to you, scribes and Pharisees, hypocrites! For you pay tithe of mint and anise and cumin, and have neglected the weightier matters of the law: justice and mercy and faith. These you ought to have done, without leaving the others undone. Blind guides, who strain out a gnat and swallow a camel! Woe to you, scribes and Pharisees, hypocrites! For you cleanse the outside of the cup and dish, but inside they are full of extortion and self-indulgence. Blind Pharisee, first cleanse the inside of the cup and dish, that the outside of them may be clean also. Woe to you, scribes and Pharisees, hypocrites! For you are like whitewashed tombs which indeed appear beautiful outwardly, but inside are full of dead men's bones and all uncleanness. Even so you also outwardly appear righteous to men, but inside you are full of hypocrisy and lawlessness. Woe to you, scribes and Pharisees, hypocrites! Because you build the tombs of the prophets and adorn the monuments of the righteous, and say, 'If we had lived in the days of our fathers, we would not have been partakers with them in the blood of the prophets.' Therefore you are witnesses against yourselves that you are sons of those who murdered the prophets. Fill up, then, the measure of your fathers' guilt. Serpents, brood of vipers! How can you escape the condemnation hell? Therefore, indeed, I send you prophets, wise men, and scribes: some of them you will kill and crucify, and some of them you will scourge in your synagogues and persecute from city to city, that on you may come all the righteous bloodshed on earth, from the blood of righteous Abel to the blood of Zechariah, son of Berechiah, whom you murdered between the temple and the altar. Assuredly, I say to you, all these things will come upon this generation. O Jerusalem, Jerusalem, the one who kills the prophets and stones those who are sent to her! How often wanted to gather your children together, as a hen gathers her chicks under her wings, but you were not willing! See! Your house is left to you desolate; for I say to you, you shall see Me no more till you say, 'Blessed is He who comes in the name of the Lord!'" (Matthew 23:1–39)

Then Jesus went out and departed from the temple, and His disciples came up to show Him the buildings of the temple. And Jesus said to them, "Do you not see all these things? Assuredly, I say to you, not one stone shall be left here upon another, that shall not be thrown down." Now as He sat on the Mount of Olives, the disciples came to Him privately, saying, "Tell us, when will these things be? And what will be the sign of Your coming, and of the end of the age?" And Jesus answered and said to them: "Take heed that no one deceives you. For many will come in My name, saying, 'I am the Christ,' and will deceive many. And you will hear of wars and rumors of wars. See that you are not troubled; for all these things must come to pass, but the end is not yet. For nation will rise against nation, and kingdom against kingdom. And there will be famines, pestilences, and earthquakes in various places. All these are the beginning of sorrows. Then they will deliver you up to tribulation and kill you, and you will be hated by all nations for My name's sake And then many will be offended, will betray one another, and will hate one another. Then many false prophets will rise up and deceive many. And because lawlessness will abound, the love of many will grow cold. But he who endures to the end shall be saved. And this gospel of the kingdom will be preached in all the world as a witness to all nations, and then the end will come. Therefore, when you see the 'abomination of desolation,' spoken of by Daniel the prophet, standing in the holy place (whoever reads, let him understand), then let those who are in Judea flee to the mountains. Let him who is on the housetop not go down to take anything out of his house. And let him who is in the field not go back to get his clothes. But woe to these who are pregnant and to those who are nursing babies in those days! And pray that your flight may not be in winter or on the Sabbath. For then

## JESUS IS GOD

there will be great tribulation, such as has not been since the beginning of the world until this time, no nor ever shall be. And unless those days were shortened, no flesh would be saved; but for the elect's sake those days will be shortened. Then if anyone says to you, 'Look, here is the Christ!' Or There!' Do not believe it. For false christs and false prophets will rise and show great signs and wonders to deceive, if possible, even the elect. See, I have told you beforehand. Therefore, if they say to you 'Look, He is in the inner rooms!' Do not believe it. For as the lightning comes from the east and flashes to the west, so also will the coming of the Son of Man be. For wherever the carcass is, there the eagles will be gathered together. Immediately after the tribulation of those days the sun will be darkened, and the moon will not give its light; the stars will fall from heaven, and the powers of the heavens will be shaken. Then the sign of the Son of Man will appear in heaven, and then all the tribes of earth will mourn, and they will see the Son of Man coming on the clouds of heaven with power and great glory. And He will send His angels with a great sound of a trumpet, and they will gather together His elect from the four winds, from one end of heaven to the other. Now learn this parable from the fig tree: When its branch has already become tender and puts forth leaves, you know that summer is near. So you also, when you see all these things, know that it is near—at the door! Assuredly, I say to you, this generation will by no means pass away till all these things take place. Heaven and earth will pass away, but My words will by no means pass away. But of that day and hour no one knows, not even the angels of heaven, but My Father only. But as the days of Noah were, so also will the coming of the Son of Man be. For as in the days before the flood, they were eating and drinking, marrying and giving in marriage, until the day that Noah entered the ark, and did not know until the flood came and took them all away, so also will the coming of the Son of Man be. Then two men will be in the field: one will be taken and the other left. Two women will be grinding at the mill: one will be taken and the other left. Watch therefore, for you do not know what hour your Lord is coming. But know this, that if the master of the house had known what hour the thief would come, he would have watched and not allowed his house to be broken into. Therefore, you also be ready, for the Son of Man is coming at an hour you do not expect. Who then is a faithful and wise servant, whom his master made ruler over his household, to give them food in due season? Blessed is that servant whom his master, when he comes, will find so doing. Assuredly, I say to you that he will make him ruler over all his goods. But if that evil servant says in his heart, 'My master's delaying his coming,' and begins to beat his fellow servants, and to eat and drink with the drunkards, the master of that servant will come on a day when he is not looking for him and at an hour that he is not aware of, and will cut him in two and appoint him his portion with the hypocrites. There shall be weeping and gnashing of teeth." (Matthew 24:1–51)

"Then the kingdom of heaven shall be likened to ten virgins who took their lamps and went out to meet the bridegroom. Now five of them were wise, and five were foolish. Those who were foolish took their lamps and took no oil with them, but the wise took oil in their vessels with their lamps. But while the bridegroom was delayed, they all slumbered and slept. And at midnight a cry was heard: 'Behold, the bridegroom is coming; go out to meet him!' Then all those virgins arose and trimmed their lamps. And the foolish said to the wise, 'Give us some of your oil, for our lamps are going out.' But the wise answered, saying, 'No lest there should not be enough for us and you; but go rather to those who sell, and buy for yourselves.' And while they went to buy, the bridegroom came, and those who were ready went in with him to the wedding; and the door was shut. Afterward the other virgins came also, saying, 'Lord, Lord, open to us!' But he answered and said, 'Assuredly, I say to you, I do not know you.'

"Watch therefore, for you know neither the day nor the hour in which the Son of Man is coming. For the kingdom of heaven is like a man traveling to a far country, who called his own servants and delivered his goods to them. And to one he gave five talents, to another two, and to another one, to each according to his own ability; and immediately he went on a journey. Then he who had received the five talents went and traded with them, and made another five talents. And likewise he who had received two gained two more also. But he who had received one went and dug in the ground, and hid his lord's money. After a long time the lord of those servants came and settled accounts with them. So he who had received five talents came and brought five other talents, saying, 'Lord, you delivered to me five talents; look, I have gained five more talents besides them.' His lord said to him, 'Well done, good and faithful servant; you were faithful over a few things, I will make you ruler over many things. Enter into the joy of your lord.' He also who had received two talents came and said, 'Lord, you delivered to me two talents; look, I have gained two more talents besides them.' His lord said to him, 'Well done, good and faithful servant; you have been faithful over a few things, I will make you ruler over many things. Enter into the joy of your lord.' Then he who had received the one talent came and said, 'Lord, I knew you to be a hard man, reaping where you have not sown, and gathering where you have not scattered seed. And I was afraid, and went and hid your talent in the ground. Look, there you have what is yours.' But his lord answered and said to him, 'You wicked and lazy servant, you knew that I reap where I have not sown, and gather where I have not scattered seed. So you ought to have deposited my money with the bankers, and at my coming I would have received back my own with interest. Therefore, take the talent from him, and give it to him who has ten talents.' For to everyone who has, more will be given, and he will have abundance; but from him who does not have, even what he has will be taken away. And cast the unprofitable servant into the outer darkness. There will be weeping and gnashing of teeth. When the Son of Man comes in His glory, and all the holy angels with Him, then He will sit on the throne of His glory. All the nations will be gathered before Him, and He will separate them one from another, as a shepherd divides his sheep from the goats. And He will set the

sheep on His right hand, but the goats on the left. Then the King will say to those on His right hand, 'Come, you blessed of My Father, inherit the kingdom prepared for you from the foundation of the world: for I was hungry and you gave Me food: I was thirsty and you gave Me drink; I was a stranger and you took Me in; I was naked and you clothed Me; I was sick and you visited Me; I was in prison and you came to Me.' Then the righteous will answer Him, saying, 'Lord, when did we see You hungry and feed You, or thirsty and give You drink? When did we see You a stranger and take You in, or naked and clothe You? Or when did we see You sick, or in prison, and come to You?' And the King will answer and say to them, 'Assuredly, I say to you, inasmuch as you did it to one of the least of these My brethren, you did it to Me.' Then He will also say to those on the left hand. 'Depart from Me, you cursed, into the everlasting fire prepared for the devil and his angels: for I was hungry and you gave Me no food; I was thirsty and you gave Me no drink; I was a stranger and you did not take Me in, naked and you did not clothe Me, sick and in prison and you did not visit Me.' Then they also will answer Him, saying, 'Lord, when did we see You hungry or thirsty or a stranger or naked or sick or in prison, and did not minister to You?' Then He will answer them, saying, 'Assuredly, I say to you, inasmuch as you did not do into one of the least of these, you'd not do it to Me.' And these will go away into everlasting punishment, but the righteous into eternal life."
(Matthew 25:1–46)

Now it came to pass, when Jesus had finished all these saying, that He said to His disciples, "You know that after two days is the Passover, and the Son of Man will be delivered up to be crucified." Then the chief priests, the scribes, and the elders of the people assembled at the palace of the high priest, who was called Caiaphas, and plotted to take Jesus by trickery and kill Him, But they said, "Not during the feast, lest there be an uproar among the people." And when Jesus was in Bethany at the house of Simon the leper, a woman came to Him having an alabaster flask of very costly fragrant oil, and she pour it on His head as He sat at the table. But when His disciples saw it, they were indignant, saying, "Why this waste? For this fragrant oil might have been sold for much and given to the poor." But when Jesus was aware of it, He said to them, "Why do you trouble the woman? For she has done a good work for Me. For you have the poor with you always, but Me you do not have always. For in pour this fragrant oil on My body, she did it for My burial. Assuredly, I say to you, wherever this gospel is preached in the whole world, what this woman has done will also be told as a memorial to her."

Then one of the twelve, called Judas Iscariot, went to the chief priests and said, "What are you willing to give me if I deliver Him to you?" And they counted out to him thirty pieces of silver. So from that time he sought opportunity to betray Him.

Now on the first day of the Feast of Unleavened Bread, the disciples came to Jesus, saying to Him, "Where do You want us to prepare for You to eat the Passover?" And He said,

# JESUS IS GOD

"Go into the city to a certain man, and say to him, 'The Teacher says, "My time is at hand; I will keep the Passover at your house with My disciples."'" So the disciples did as Jesus had directed them; and they prepared the Passover. When evening had come, He sat down with the twelve. Now as they were eating, He said, "Assuredly, I say to you, one of you will betray Me." And they were exceedingly sorrowful, and each of them began to say to Him, "Lord, is it I?" He answered and said, "He who dipped his hand with Me in the dish will betray Me. The Son of Man indeed goes just as it is written of Him, but woe to that man by whom the Son of Man is betrayed! It would have been good for that man if he had not been born." Then Judas, who was betraying Him, answered and said, "Rabbi, is it I?" He said to him, "You have said it." And as they were eating, Jesus took bread, blessed and broke it, and gave it to the disciples and said, "Take, eat; this is My body." Then He took the cup, and gave thanks, and gave it to them, saying, "Drink from it, all of you. For this is My blood of the new covenant, which is shed for many for the remission of sins. But I say to you, I will not drink of this fruit of the vine from now on until that day when I drink it new with you in My Father's kingdom."

And when they had sung a hymn, they went out to the Mount of Olives. Then Jesus said to them, "All of you will be made to stumble because of Me this night, for it is written: 'I will strike the Shepherd, And the sheep of the flock will be scattered.' But after I have been raised, I will go before you to Galilee." Peter answered and said to Him, "Even if all are made to stumble because of You, I will never be made to stumble."

Jesus said to him, "Assuredly, I say to you that this night, before the rooster crows, you will deny Me three times." Peter said to Him, "Even if I have to die with You, I will not deny You!" And so said all the disciples.

Then Jesus came with them to a place called Gethsemane, and said to the disciples, "Sit here while I go and pray over there." And He took with Him Peter and the two sons of Zebedee, and He began to be sorrowful and deeply distressed. Then He said to them, "My soul is exceeding sorrowful, even to death. Stay here and watch with Me." He went a little farther and fell on His face and prayed, saying, "O My Father, if it is possible, let this cup pass from Me; nevertheless, not as I will but as You will." Then He came to the disciples and found them sleeping, and said to Peter, "What? Could you not watch with Me one hour? What and pray, lest you enter into temptation. The spirit indeed is willing, but the flesh is weak." Again, a second time, He went away and prayed, saying, "O My Father, if this cup cannot pass away from Me unless Drink it, Your will be done." And He came and found them asleep again, for their eyes were heavy. So He left them, went away again, and prayed the third time, saying the same words. Then He came to His disciples and said to them, "Are you still sleeping and resting? Behold, the hour is at hand, and the Son of Man is being betrayed into the hands of sinners. Rise, let us be going. See, My betrayer is at hand." And while He was still speaking, behold, Judas, one of the twelve, with a great multitude with swords and clubs, came from the chief priests and elder of the people. Now His betrayer had given them a sign, saying, "Whomever I

## JESUS IS GOD

kiss, He is the One; seize Him." Immediately, he went up to Jesus and said, "Greeting, Rabbi!" and kissed Him. But Jesus said to him, "Friend, why have you come?" Then they came and laid hands on Jesus and took Him. And suddenly, one of those who were with Jesus stretched out his hand and drew his sword, struck the servant of the high priest, and cut off his ear. But Jesus said to him, "Put your sword in its place, for all who take the sword will perish by the sword. Or do you think that I cannot now pray to My Father, and He will provide Me with more than twelve legions of angels? How then could the Scripture be fulfilled, that it must happen thus?" In that hour Jesus said to the multitude, "Have you come out, as against a robber, with swords and clubs to take Me? I sat daily with you, teaching in the temple, and you did not seize Me. But all this was done that the Scriptures of the prophets might be fulfilled."

Then all the disciples forsook Him and fled. And those who had laid hold of Jesus led Him away to Caiaphas, the high priest, where the scribes and the elder were assembled. But Peter followed Him at a distance to the high priest's courtyard. And he went in and sat with the servants to see the end. Now the chief priests, the elders, and all the council sought false testimony against Jesus to put Him to death, but found none. Even though many false witnesses came forward, they found none. But at last two false witnesses came forward and said, "This fellow said, 'I am able to destroy the temple of God and to build it in three days.'" And the high priest arose and said to Him, "Do You answer nothing? What is it these men testify against

You?" But Jesus kept silent. And the high priest answered and said to Him, "I put You under oath by the living God: tell us if You are the Christ, the Son of God!" Jesus said to him, "It is as you said. Nevertheless, I say to you, hereafter you will see the Son of Man sitting at the right hand of the Power, and coming on the clouds of heaven." Then the high priest tore his clothes, saying, "He has spoken blasphemy! What further need do we have of witnesses? Look, now you have heard His blasphemy! What do you think?" They answered and said, He is deserving of death." Then they spat in His face and beat Him; and other struck Him with the palms of their hands, saying, "Prophesy to us, Christ! Who is the one who struck You?"

Now Peter sat outside in the courtyard. And a servant girl came to him, saying, "You also were with Jesus of Galilee." But he denied it before them all, saying, "I do not know what you are saying." And when he had gone out to the gateway, another girl saw him and said to those who were there, "This fellow also was with Jesus of Nazareth." But again he denied with an oath, "I do not know the Man!" And a little later those who stood by came up and said to Peter, "Surely you also are one of them, for your speech betrays you." Then he began to curse and swear, saying, "I do not know the Man!" Immediately, a rooster crowed. And Peter remembered the word of Jesus who had said to him, "Before the rooster crows, you will deny Me three times." So he went out and wept bitterly. (Matthew 26: 1–75)

# CHAPTER 9

## Scripture References about God the Holy Spirit

If you love Me, keep My commandments. And I will pray the Father, and He will give you another Helper, that He may abide with you forever—he Spirit of truth, whom they would cannot receive, because it neither sees Him nor knows Him; but you know Him, for He dwells with you and will be in you. I will not leave you orphans; I will come to you. (John 14:15–18)

But the Helper, the Holy Spirit, whom the Father will send in My name, He will teach you all things, and bring to your remembrance all things that I said to you. (John 14:26)

But when the Helper comes, whom I shall send to you from the Father, the Spirit of truth who proceeds from the Father, He will testify of Me. (John 15:26)

God the Holy Spirit participated in creation.

> The earth was without form, and void; and darkness was on the face of the deep. And the Spirit of God was hovering over the face of the waters. (Genesis 1:2)

> Until the Spirit is poured upon us from on high, And the wilderness becomes a fruitful field, and the fruitful field is counted as a forest. (Isaiah 32:15)

The Spirit gives life to humanity.

> You send forth Your Spirit, they are created; and You renew the face of the earth. (Psalm 104:30)

> And the Lord God formed man of the dust of the ground, and breathed into his nostrils the breath of life; and man became a living being. (Genesis 2:7)

> And the Lord said, My Spirit shall not strive with man forever, for he is indeed flesh; yet his days shall be one hundred and twenty years. (Genesis 6:3)

The Spirit came upon certain judges, warriors, and prophets in a way that gave them extraordinary power. For example,

*Joshua*

> And the Lord said to Moses: "Take Joshua, the son of Nun, with you, a man in whom is the

Spirit, and lay your hand on him." (Numbers 27:18)

*Gideon*

But the Spirit of the Lord came upon Gideon; then he blew the trumpet, and the Abiezrites gathered behind him. (Judges 6:34)

*Samson*

So the woman bore a son and called his name Samson; and the child grew, and the Lord blessed him. And the Spirit of the Lord began to move upon him at Mahaneh Dan between Zorah and Eshtaol. (Judges 13:24–25)

And the Spirit of the Lord came mightily upon him, and he tore the lion apart as one would have torn apart a young goat, though he had nothing in his hand. But he did not tell his father or his mother what he had done. (Judges 14:6)

*Saul*

Then the Spirit of the Lord will come upon you, and you will prophesy with them and be turned into another man. And let it be, when these sign come to you, that you do as the occasion demands; for God is with you. (1 Samuel 10:6, 7)

When they came there to the hill, there was a group of prophets to meet him; then the

Spirit of God came upon him, and he prophesied among them. (1 Samuel 10:10)

*Othniel*

> When the children of Israel cried out to the Lord, the Lord raised up a deliverer for the children of Israel, who delivered them: Othniel the son of Kenaz, Caleb's younger brother. The Spirit of the Lord came upon him, and he judged Israel. He went out to war, and the Lord delivered Cushan-Rishathaim, king of Mesopotamia, into his hand; and his hand prevailed over Cushan-Rishathaim. (Judges 3:9–10)

God the Holy Spirit played a prominent role in the entire span of the Old Testament prophecy.

> The Spirit of the Lord spoke by me, And His word was on my tongue. The God of Israel said, The Rock of Israel spoke to me: "He who rules over men must be just, ruling in the fear of God." (2 Samuel 23:2–3)

> Then the Spirit entered me when He spoke to me, and set me on my feet; and I heard Him who spoke to me. And He said to me: "Son of Man, I am sending you to the children of Israel, to a rebellious nation that has rebelled against Me; they and their fathers have transgressed against Me to this very day. For they are impudent and stubborn children. I am sending you to them, and you shall say to them, 'Thus says the Lord God.'" (Ezekiel 2:2–4)

God the Holy Spirit inspired holiness in the Old Testament believers.

> Teach me to do Your will, for You are my God; Your Spirit is good. Lead me in the land of uprightness. (Psalm 143:10)

Scripture promised that someday God would put His Spirit in His people, in a way that would cause them to live according to His statutes.

> I will put My Spirit within you and cause you to walk in My statues, and you will keep My judgments and do them. Then you shall dwelling the land that I gave to your father; you shall be My people, and I will be your God. (Ezekiel 36:27–28)

God the Holy Spirit was crucial in helping God's people anticipate the ministry of the Messiah, Jesus.

> There shall come forth a Rod from the stem of Jesse, and a branch shall grow out of his roots. The Spirit of the Lord shall rest upon Him, The Spirit of wisdom and understanding, The Spirit of counsel and might, The Spirit of knowledge and of the fear of the Lord. His delight is in the fear of the Lord, and He shall not judge by the sight of His eyes, nor decide by the hearing of His ears; but with righteousness He shall judge the poor, and decide with equity for the meek of the earth; He shall strike the earth with the rod of His mouth, And with the breath of His lips He shall slay the wicked. Righteousness shall be the belt of His loins, and faithfulness the belt of His waist. (Isaiah 11:1–5)

In a Trinitarian preview of the working of God the Father; God the Holy Spirit; and God the Son (Jesus), who is the Branch of Jesse, looking forward to the ministry of Jesus Christ, God the Holy Spirit inspired Isaiah to prophesy, "The Spirit of the Lord shall rest upon Him," as mentioned in Isaiah 11:2, giving God's Chosen One wisdom, fear of the Lord, righteousness, and faithfulness. Thus, we come full circle to the New Testament, where Jesus claimed to be the fulfillment of this prophecy.

> The Spirit of the Lord God is upon Me, because the Lord has anointed Me to preach good tidings to the poor; He has sent Me to heal the brokenhearted, to proclaim liberty to the captives, and the opening of the prison to those who are bound; to proclaim the acceptable year of the Lord, and the day of vengeance of our God; to comfort all who mourn, to console those who mourn in Zion, to give them beauty for ashes, the oil of joy for mourning, the garment of praise for the spirit of heaviness; that they may be called trees of righteousness, the planting of the Lord, that He may be glorified. (Isaiah 61:1–3)

In parallel to these scriptures in the Old Testament, Luke explains the matter further with God the Son (Jesus) at that time on earth, starting in Luke 4:14–21:

> Then Jesus returned in the power of the Spirit to Galilee, and news of Him went out through all the surrounding region. And He taught in their synagogues, being glorified by all. So He came to Nazareth, where He had been brought up. And as His custom was, He went into the synagogue on the Sabbath day, and stood up to read. And He was handed the book of the prophet Isaiah. And when He had opened

## JESUS IS GOD

the book, He found the place where it was written: "The Spirit of the Lord is upon Me, because He has anointed Me, to preach the gospel to the poor; He has sent Me to heal the brokenhearted, to proclaim liberty to the captives and recovery of sight to the blind, to set at liberty those who are oppressed; to proclaim the acceptable year of the Lord." Then He closed the book, and gave it back to the attendant and sat down. And the eyes of all who were in the synagogue were fixed on Him. And He began to say to them, "Today this Scripture is fulfilled in your hearing."

Now let's continue to explore the Holy Bible featuring scriptures about God the Holy Spirit.

> Now the birth of Jesus Christ was as follows: after His mother Mary was betrothed to Joseph, before they came together, she was found with child of the Holy Spirit. (Matthew 1:18)

> But while he thought about these things, behold, an angel of the Lord appeared to him in a dream, saying, "Joseph, son of David, do not be afraid to take to you Mary, your wife, for that which is conceived in her is of the Holy Spirit." (Matthew 1:20)

> Therefore I say to you, every sin and blasphemy will be forgiven men, but the blasphemy against the Spirit will not be forgiven men. (Matthew 12:31)

> I indeed baptized you with water, but He will baptize you with the Holy Spirit. (Mark 1:8)

*Assuredly, I say to you, all sins will be forgiven the sons of men, and whatever blasphemies they may utter; but he who blasphemes against the Holy Spirit never has forgiveness, but is subject to eternal condemnation.* (Mark 3:28–29)

*For David himself said by the Holy Spirit: "The Lord said to my Lord, 'Sit at My right hand till I make Your enemies Your footstool.'"* (Mark 12:36)

*But when they arrest you and deliver you up, do not worry beforehand, or premeditate what you will speak. But whatever is given you in that hour, speak that; for it is not you who will speak, but the Holy Spirit.* (Mark 13:11)

For he will be great in the sight of the Lord, and shall drink neither wine nor strong drink. He will also be filled with the Holy Spirit, even from his mother's womb. (Luke 1:15)

And the angel answered and said to her, "The Holy Spirit will came upon you, and the power of the Highest will overshadow you; therefore, also that Holy One who is to be born will be called the Son of God." (Luke 1:35)

And it happened, when Elizabeth heard the greeting of Mary, that the babe leaped in her womb; and Elizabeth was filled with the Holy Spirit. Then she spoke out with a loud voice and said, "Blessed are you among women, and blessed is the fruit of your womb!" (Luke 1:41–42)

Now his father Zachary's was filled with the Holy Spirit, and prophesied, saying: "Blessed is the Lord God of Israel, for He has visited and redeemed His people, and has raised up a horn of salvation for us in the house of His servant David, as He spoke by the mouth of His holy prophets, Who have been since the world began." (Luke 1:67–70)

And behold, there was a man in Jerusalem whose name was Simeon, and this man was just and devout, waiting for the Consolation of Israel, and the Holy Spirit was upon him. And it had been revealed to him by the Holy Spirit that he would not see death before he had seen the Lord's Christ. So he came by the Spirit into the temple. And when the parents brought in the Child Jesus, to do for Him according to the custom of the law. ( Luke 2:25–27)

John answered, saying to all, "I indeed baptize you with water; but One mightier than I is coming, whose sandal strap I am not worthy to loose. He will baptize you with the Holy Spirit and fire." (Luke 3:16)

Then Jesus, being filled with the Holy Spirit, returned from the Jordan and was led by the Spirit into the wilderness. (Luke 4:1)

And anyone who speaks a word against the Son of Man, it will be forgiven him; but to him who blasphemes against the Holy Spirit, it will not be forgiven. (Luke 12:10)

*For the Holy Spirit will teach you in that very hour what you ought to say.* (Luke 12:12)

I did not know Him, but He who sent me to baptize with water said to me, "Upon whom you see the Spirit descending, and remaining on Him, this is He who baptizes with the Holy Spirit." And I have seen and testified that this is the Son of God. (John 1:33–34)

On the last day, that great day of the feast, Jesus stood and cried out, saying, *"If anyone thirsts, let him come to Me and drink. He who believes in Me, as the Scripture has said, out of his heart will flow rivers of living water."* But this He spoke concerning the Spirit, whom those believing in Him would receive; for the Holy Spirit was not yet given, because Jesus was not yet glorified. (John 7:37–39)

So Jesus said to them again, *"Peace to you! As the Father has sent Me, I also send you."* And when He had said this, He breathed on them and said to them, *"Receive the Holy Spirit."* (John 20:21–22)

Until the day in which He was taken up, after He through the Holy Spirit had given commandments to the apostles whom He had chosen. (Acts 1:2)

*For John truly baptized with water, but you shall be baptized with the Holy Spirit not many days from now.* (Acts 1:5)

> But you shall receive power when the Holy Spirit has come upon you; and you shall be witnesses to Me in Jerusalem, and in all Judea and Samaria, and to the end of the earth. (Acts 1:8)

Men and brethren, this Scripture had to be fulfilled, which the Holy Spirit spoke before by the mouth of David concerning Judas, who became a guide to those who arrested Jesus. (Acts 1:16)

And they were all filled with the Holy Spirit and began to speak with other tongues, as the Spirit gave them utterance. (Acts 2:4)

Then Peter said to them, "Repent, and let every one of you be baptized in the name of Jesus Christ for the remission of sins; and you shall receive the gift of the Holy Spirit." (Acts 2:38)

Then Peter, filled with the Holy Spirit, said to them, "Rulers of the people and elders of Israel: if we this day are judged for a good deed done to a helpless man, by what means he has been made well, let it be known to you all, and to all the people of Israel, that by the name of Jesus Christ of Nazareth, whom you crucified, whom God raised from the dead, by Him this man stands here before you whole." (Acts 4:8–10)

And when they had prayed, the place where they were assembled together was shaken; and they were all filled with the Holy Spirit, and they spoke the word of God with boldness. (Acts 4:31)

But Peter said, "Ananias, why has satan filled you heart to lie to the Holy Spirit and keep back part of the price of the land for yourself?" (Acts 5:3)

And we are His witnesses to these things, and so also is the Holy Spirit whom God has given to those who obey Him. (Acts 5:32)

Therefore, brethren, seek out from among you seven men of good reputation, full of the Holy Spirit and wisdom, whom we may appoint over this business. (Acts 6:3)

And the saying pleased the whole multitude. And they chose Stephen, a man full of faith and the Holy Spirit, and Phillip, Prochorus, Nicanor, Timon, Parmenas, and Nicolas, a proselyte from Antioch. (Acts 6:5)

You stiff-necked and uncircumcised in heart and ears! You always resist the Holy Spirit; as your fathers did, so do you. (Acts 7:51)

Who, when they had come down, prayed for them that they might receive the Holy Spirit. (Acts 8:15)

Then they laid hands on them, and they received the Holy Spirit. And when Simon saw that through the laying on of the apostle hands the Holy Spirit was given, he offered them money, saying, "Give me this power also, that anyone on whom I lay hands may receive the Holy Spirit." But Peter said to him, "Your money perish with

## JESUS IS GOD

you, because you thought that the gift of God could be purchased with money!" (Acts 8:17–20)

Now there was a certain disciple at Damascus named Ananias; and to him the Lord said in a vision, "Ananias." And he said, "Here I am, Lord." So the Lord said to him, "Arise and go to the street called Straight, and inquire at the house of Judas for one called Saul of Tarsus, for behold, he is praying. And in a vision he has seen a man named Ananias coming in and putting his hand on him, so that he might receive his sight." Then Ananias answered, "Lord, I have heard from many about this man, how much harm he has done to Your saints in Jerusalem. And here he has authority from the chief priests to bind all who call on your name." But the Lord said to him, "Go, for he is a chosen vessel of Mine to bear My name before the Gentiles, kings, and the children of Israel. For I will show him how many things he must offer for My name's sake." And Ananias went his way and entered the house; and laying his hands on him, he said, "Brother Saul, the Lord Jesus, who appeared to you on the road as you came, has sent me that you may receive your sight and be filled with the Holy Spirit." Immediately, there fell from his eyes something like scales, and he received his sight at once; and he arose and was baptized. (Acts 9:10–18)

Then the churches throughout all Judea, Galilee, and Samaria had peace and were edified. And walking in the fear of the Lord and in the comfort of the Holy Spirit, they were multiplied. (Acts 9:31s)

While Peter was still speaking these words, the Holy Spirit fell upon all those who heard the word. And those of the circumcision who believed were astonished, as many as came with Peter, because the gift of the Holy Spirit had been poured out on the Gentiles also. For they heard them speak with tongues and magnify God. Then Peter answered, "Can anyone forbid water, that these should not be baptized who have received the Holy Spirit just as we have?" And he commanded them to be baptized in the name of the Lord. Then they asked him to stay a few days. (Acts 10:44-48)

And as I began to speak, the Holy Spirit fell upon them, as upon us at the beginning. Then I remembered the word of the Lord, how He said, "John indeed baptized with water, but you shall be baptized with the Holy Spirit." (Acts 11:15–16)

For he was a good man, full of the Holy Spirit and of faith. And a great many people were added to the Lord. (Acts 11:24)

As they ministered to the Lord and fasted, the Holy Spirit said, "Now separate to Me Barnabas and Saul for the work to which I have called them." Then, having fasted and prayed, and laid hands on them, they sent them away. So, being sent out by the Holy Spirit, they went down to Seleucia, and from there they sailed to Cyprus. (Acts 13:2–4)

Then Saul, who also is called Paul, filled with the Holy Spirit, looked intently at him! (Acts 13:9)

And the disciples were filled with joy and with the Holy Spirit. (Acts 13:52)

So God, who knows the heart, acknowledged them by giving them the Holy Spirit, just as He did to us, and made no distinction between us and them, purifying theirs hearts by faith. (Acts 15:8–9)

For it seemed good to the Holy Spirit, and to us, to lay upon you no greater burden than these necessary things: that you abstain from things offered to idols, from blood, from things strangled, and from sexual immorality. If you keep yourselves from these, you will do well. (Acts 15:28–29)

Now when they had gone through Phrygia and the region of Galatia, they were forbidden by the Holy Spirit to preach the word in Asia. After they had come to Mysia, they tried to go into Bithynia, but the Spirit did not permit them. (Acts 16:6–7)

And it happened, while Apollos was at Corinth, that Paul, having passed through the upper regions, came to Ephesus. And finding some disciples he said to them, "Did you receive the Holy Spirit when you believed?" So they said to him, "We have not so much as heard whether there is a Holy Spirit." And he said to them, "Into so they said, into John's baptism." Then Paul said, "John indeed baptized with a baptism of repentance, saying to the people that they should believe on Him who would come after him that is, on Christ Jesus." When they heard this, they were baptized in the name of the Lord Jesus. And when Paul had laid hands on them, the Holy Spirit came upon them, and they spoke with tongues and prophesied. Now the men were about twelve in all. (Acts 19:1–7)

And see, now I go bound in the Spirit to Jerusalem, not knowing the things that will happen to me there, except that the Holy Spirit testifies in every city, saying that chains and tribulations await me. But none of these things move me; nor do I count my life dear to myself, so that I may finish my race with joy, and the ministry which I received from the Lord Jesus, to testify to the gospel of the grace of God. (Acts 20:22–24)

When he had come to us, he took Paul's belt, bound his own hands and feet, and said, "Thus says the Holy Spirit, 'So shall the Jews at Jerusalem bind the man who owns the belt, and deliver him into the hands of the Gentiles.'" (Acts 21:11)

So when they did not agree among themselves, they departed after Paul had said on word: "Holy Spirit spoke rightly through Isaiah the prophet to our fathers, saying, 'Go to this people and say: "Hearing you will hear, and shall not understand; And seeing you will see, and not perceive: For the hearts of this people have grown dull. Their ears are hard of hearing, And their eyes they have closed, Lest they should see with their eyes and hear with their ears, Lest they should understand with their hearts and turn. So that I should heal them."'" (Acts 28:25)

I tell the truth in Christ, I am not lying, my conscience also bearing me witness in the Holy Spirit. (Romans 9:1)

Therefore, do not let your good be spoken of as evil; for the kingdom of God is not eating and drinking, but righteousness and peace and joy in the Holy Spirit. (Roman's 14:16–17)

Now may the God of hope fill you with all joy and peace in believing, that you may abound in hope by the power of the Holy Spirit. Now I myself am confident concerning you, my brethren, that you also are full of goodness, filled with all knowledge, able also to admonish one another. Nevertheless, brethren, I have written more boldly to you on some points, as reminding you, because of the grace given to me by God, that I might be a minister of Jesus Christ to the Gentiles, ministering the gospel of God, that the offering of the Gentiles might be acceptable, sanctified by the Holy Spirit. Therefore, I have reason to glory in Christ Jesus in the things which pertain to God. (Romans 15:13–17)

These things we also speak, not in words which man's wisdom teaches but which the Holy Spirit teaches, comparing spiritual things with spiritual. But the natural man does not receive the things of the Spirit of God, for they are foolish ness to him; nor can he know them, because they are spiritually discerned. (1 Corinthians 2:13–14)

But he who is joined to the Lord is one spirit with Him. Flee sexual immorality. Every sin that a man does is outside the body, but he who commits sexual immorality sins against his own body. Or do you not know that your body is the temple of the Holy Spirit who is in you, whom you have from God, and you are not your own? For you were bought at a price; therefore glorify God in your body and in your spirit, which are God's. (1 Corinthians 6:17–20)

Therefore, I make known to you that no one speaking by the Spirit of God calls Jesus accused, and no one can say that Jesus is Lord except by the Holy Spirit. (1 Corinthians 12:3)

By purity, by knowledge, by long-suffering, by kindness, by the Holy Spirit, by sincere love. (2 Corinthians 6:6)

For our gospel did not come to you in word only, but also in power, and in the Holy Spirit and in much assurance, as you know what kind of men we were among you for your sake. And you because followers of us and of the Lord, having received the word in much affliction, with joy of the Holy Spirit. (1 Thessalonians 1:5–6)

Hold fast the pattern of sound words which you have heard from me, in faith and love which are in Christ Jesus. That good thing which was committed to you, keep by the Holy Spirit who dwelling us. (2 Timothy 1:14)

But when the kindness and the love of God our Savior toward man appeared, not by works of righteousness which we have done, but according to His mercy He saved us, through the washing of regeneration and renewing of the Holy Spirit, whom He poured out on us abundantly through Jesus Christ our Savior, that having been justified by His grace we should become heirs according to the hope of eternal life. (Titus 3:4–7)

How shall we escape if we neglect so great a salvation, which at the first began to be spoken by the Lord, and was confirmed to us by those who heard Him, God also bearing witness both with signs and wonders, with various miracles, and gifts of the Holy Spirit, according to His own will? (Hebrews 2:3–4)

Therefore, as the Holy Spirit says: "Today, if you will hear His voice, do not harden your hearts as in the rebellion, in the day of trial in the wilderness, where your fathers tested Me, tried Me, and saw My works forty years. Therefore, I was angry with that generation, and said 'They always go astray in their heart, and they have not known My ways.' So I swore in My wrath, 'They shall not enter My rest.'" Beware, brethren, lest there be in any of you an evil heart of unbelief in departing from the living God; but exhort one another daily, while it is called "Today," lest any of you be hardened through the deceitfulness of sin for we have become partakers of Christ if we hold the beginning of our confidence steadfast to the end. (Hebrews 3:7–14)

For it is impossible for those who were once enlighten, and have tasted the heavenly gift, and have become partakers of the Holy Spirit, and have tasted the good word of God and the powers of the age to come, if they fall away, to renew them again to repentance, since they crucify again for themselves the Son of God, and put Him to an open shame. For the earth which drinks in the rain that often comes upon it, and bears herbs useful for those by whom it is cultivated, receives blessing from God. (Hebrews 6:4–7)

The Holy Spirit indicating this, that the way into the Holiest of All was not yet made manifest while the first tabernacle was still standing. (Hebrews 9:8)

But this Man, after He had offered one sacrifice for sins forever, sat down at the right hand of God, from that time waiting till His enemies are made His foot stool. For by one offering He has perfected forever those who are being sanctified. But the Holy Spirit also witnesses to us; for after He had said before, "This is the covenant that I will make with them after those days, says the Lord: I will put My laws into their hearts, and in their minds I will write them," then He adds, "Their sins and their lawless deeds I will remember no more," Now where there is remission of these there is no longer an offing of sin. Therefore, brethren, having boldness to enter the Holiest by the blood of Jesus, by a new and living way which He consecrated for us, through the veil, that is, His flesh, and having a High Priest over the house of God. (Hebrews 10:12–21)

To them it was revealed that, not to themselves, but to us they were ministering the things which now have been reported to you through those who have preached the gospel to you by the

Holy Spirit sent from heaven things which angels desire to look into. Therefore, gird up the loins of your mind, be sober, and rest your hope fully upon the grace that is to be brought to you at the revelation of Jesus Christ. (1 Peter 1:12–13)

For prophecy never came by the will of man, but holy men of God spoke as they were moved by the Holy Spirit. (2 Peter 1:21)

# CHAPTER 10

## Jesus Is God throughout the Bible with Key Scriptures That Show He Is God

Genesis 1:26–27 says,

> Then God said, "Let Us make man in Our image, according to Our likeness; let them have dominion over the fish of the sea, over the birds of the air, and over the cattle, over all the earth and over every creeping thing that creeps on the earth." So God created man in His own image; in the image of God He created him; male and female He created them.

In this book, I wanted to give very minimal dialogue in an effort to let the Bible speak for itself; however, here there are a few things I would like to point out. First, earlier in chapter 5, it has been established that God is God the Father; God the Son, Jesus Christ, the Anointed One; and God the Holy Spirit. In the beginning of verse 26, it says, "Then God said, 'Let US make man in Our image according to Our likeness." The word *us* (first person plural) is used by a speaker to refer to himself and one or more other people as the object of a verb or preposition. The word *our* means belonging to or associated with the speaker and one or more people. I give these definitions so that you know that the Trinity existed even all the way in the front of the Bible. The word *Genesis* means the beginning or origin. The verse also shows that humans were created in the image of God's likeness. The main thing in verse 27 that I want to point out is that God created them male and female. In verse 28, it says, "Then God blessed them, and God said to them be fruitful and multiply; fill the earth." I just want to point out here that only a man and a woman can create children, if God allows it. There's is no other way but the way God ordained for it to be.

Genesis 3:14–15 says,

> So the Lord God said to the serpent: "Because you have done this, You are cured more than all cattle, And more than every beast of the field; on your belly you shall go, And you shall eat dust all the days your life. And I will put enmity between you and the woman, and between your seed and her Seed; He shall bruise your head, and you shall bruise His heel."

What I would like for you to glean from these two scriptures as it relates to Jesus Christ is that in verse 15, God said, "I will put enmity between you and the woman, and between your seed and her Seed." First of all, a woman does not produce seed, she produces eggs, not sperm or seed. Next, the word *Seed* here starts with a capital letter indicating this is God. All throughout the Bible, anytime God the Father or God the Son or God the Holy Spirit is written in the Bible, it starts with a capital letter. This was God telling Satan (represented here as a serpent) that Jesus was coming to the world. Satan came to the woman (Eve) in the form of a snake. Satan bruised Jesus's heel by having him crucified on a cross. However, Jesus bruised his head by defeating death, sin, and the grave by rising from the dead on the third day. Jesus defeated the serpent at the cross, crushing his head, and winning back the world (Colossians 2:14–15) for whosoever will believe in Jesus (Romans 10:13).

Genesis 3:22 says, "Then the Lord God said, 'Behold, the man has become like one of Us, to know good and evil."

What I would like you to see here is that the scripture says, "The man has become like one of Us," Again, this shows the presence of the Trinity—God the Father, God the Son (Jesus), and God the Holy Spirit.

> For unto us a Child is born, Unto us a Son is given; and the government will be upon His shoulder. And His name will be called Wonderful, Counselor, Mighty God, Everlasting Father, Prince of Peace. Of the increase of His government and peace there will be no end, upon the throne of David and over His kingdom, To order it and establish it with judgment and justice From that time forward, even forever. The zeal of the Lord of host will perform this. (Isaiah 9:6–7)

> "Behold, the virgin shall be with child, and bear a Son, and they shall call His name Immanuel," which is translated, "God with us." (Matthew 1:23)

> Therefore the Lord Himself will give you a sign: Behold, the virgin shall conceive and bear a Son, and shall call His name Immanuel. (Isaiah 7:14)

> "I am the Alpha and the Omega, the Beginning and the End," says the Lord, "who is and who was and who is to come, the Almighty." (Revelation 1:8)

> Thus says the Lord, the King of Israel, and his Redeemer, the Lord of hosts: "I am the First and I am the Last; besides Me there is no God." (Isaiah 44:6)

## JESUS IS GOD

Jesus Christ is the same yesterday, today, and forever. (Hebrews 13:8)

But you, Bethlehem Ephrathah, though you are little among the thousands of Judah, yet out of you shall come forth to Me The One to be ruler in Israel, whose goings forth are from of old, from everlasting. (Micah 5:2)

Before the mountains were brought forth, or ever You had formed the earth and the world, even from everlasting to everlasting, You are God. (Psalm 90:2)

I was watching in the night visions, And behold, One like the Son of Man, Coming with the clouds of heaven! He came to the Ancient of Days, and they brought Him near before Him. Then to Him was given dominion and glory and a kingdom, that all people, nations, and languages should serve Him. His dominion is an everlasting dominion, which shall not pass away, and His kingdom the one which shall not be destroyed. (Daniel 7:13–14)

The Father loves the Son, and has given all things into His hand. He who believes in the Son has everlasting life; and he who does not believe the Son shall not see life, but the wrath of God abides on him. (John 3:35–36)

I will make the lame a remnant, and the outcast a strong nation; so the Lord will reign over them in Mount Zion from now on, even forever. (Micah 4:7)

Tell and bring forth your case; yes, let them take counsel together, who has declared this from ancient time? Who has told it from that time? Have not I, the Lord? And there is no other God besides Me, a just God and a Savior; there is none besides Me. Look to Me, and be saved, all you ends of the earth! For I am God, and there is no other. I have sworn by Myself; the word has gone out of My mouth in righteousness, and shall not return, that to Me every knee shall bow, every tongue shall take an oath. (Isaiah 45:21–23)

Therefore, God also has highly exalted Him and given Him the name which is above every name, that at the name of Jesus every knee should bow, of those in heaven, and of those on the earth, and of those under the earth, and that every tongue should confess that Jesus Christ is Lord, to the glory of God the Father. (Philippians 2:9–11)

All the ends of the world shall remember and turn to the Lord, And all the families of the nations shall worship before You. For the kingdom is the Lord's, and He rules over the nations. (Psalm 22:27–28)

Who has believed our report? And to whom has the arm of the Lord been revealed? For He shall grow up before Him as a tender plant, And as a root out of dry ground. He has no form or comeliness; and when we see Him, There is no beauty that we should desire Him. He is despised and rejected by men, a Man of sorrows and acquainted with grief. And we hid, as it were, our faces from Him; He was despised, and we did not esteem Him. Surely He has borne our griefs and carried our sorrows; yet we esteemed Him stricken, smitten by God, and afflicted. But He was wounded for our transgressions, He was bruised for our iniquities; the chastisement for our peace was upon Him. And by His stripe we are healed. All we like sheep have gone astray; we have turned, every one, to his own way; and the Lord has laid on Him the iniquity of us all. He was oppressed and He was afflicted, yet He opened not His mouth; He was led as a lamb to the slaughter, And as a sheep before its shearers is silent, So He opened not His mouth. He was taken from prison and from judgment, And who will declare His generation? For He was cut off from the land of the living; For the transgressions of My people He was stricken. And they made His grave with the wicked—But with the rich at His death, Because He had done no violence, Nor was any deceit in His mouth. Yet it pleased the Lord to bruise Him; He has put Him to grief. When You make His soul an offering for sin, He shall see His seed, He shall prolong His days, and the pleasure of the Lord shall prosper in His hand. He shall see the labor of His soul, and be satisfied. By His knowledge My righteous Servant shall justify many, for He shall bear their iniquities. Therefore, I will divide Him a portion with the great, and He shall divide the spoil with the strong, because He poured out His soul unto death, and He was numbered with the transgressors, And He bore the sin of many, and made intercession for the transgressors. (Isaiah 53:1–12)

Rejoice greatly, O daughter of Zion! Shout, O daughter of Jerusalem! Behold, your King is coming to you; He is just and having salvation, Lowly and riding on a donkey, a colt, the foal of a donkey. (Zechariah 9:9)

I will open my mouth in a parable; I will utter dark saying of old, which we have heard and known, and our father have told us. We will not hide them from their children, telling to the generation to come the praises of the Lord, and His strength and His wonderful works that He has done. (Psalm 78:2–4)

And the disciples came and said to Him, "Why do You speak to them in parables?" He answered and said to them, "Because it has been given to you to know the mysteries of the kingdom of heaven, but to them it has not been given." (Matthew 13:10–11)

And the inscription of His accusation was written above: THE KING OF THE JEWS. With Him they also crucified two robbers, one on His right and the other on His left. So the Scripture was fulfilled which says, "And He was numbered with the transgressors." (Mark 15:26–28)

They also gave me gall of my food, and for my thirst they gave me vinegar to drink. (Psalm 69:21)

They gave Him sour wine mingled with gall to drink. But when He had tasted it, He would not drink. (Matthew 27:34)

And I will pour on the house of David and on the inhabitants of Jerusalem the Spirit of grace and supplication; then they will look on Me whom they pierced. Yes, they will mourn for Him as one mourns for his only son, and grieve for Him as one grieves for a firstborn. (Zechariah 12:10)

Now Thomas, called the Twin, one of the twelve, was not with them when Jesus came. The other disciples therefore said to him, "We have seen the Lord." So he said to them, "Unless I see in His hands the print of the nails, and put my finger into the print of the nails, and put my hand into His side, I will not believe." And after eight days His disciples were again inside, and Thomas with them. Jesus came, the doors being shut, and stood in the midst, and said, "Peace to you!" Then He said to Thomas, "Reach your finger here, and look at My hands; and reach your hand here, and put it into My side. Do not be unbelieving, but believing." And Thomas answered and said to Him, "My Lord and my God!" Jesus said to him, "Thomas, because you have seen Me, you have believed. Blessed are those who have not seen and yet have believed." And truly Jesus did many other signs in the presence His disciples, which are not written in this book; but these are written that you may believe that Jesus is the Christ, the Son of God, and that believing you may have life in His name. (John 20:24–30)

They divide My garments among them, and for My clothing they cast lots. (Psalm 22:18)

Then Jesus said, "Father, forgive them, for they do not know what they do." And they divided His garments and cast lots. (Luke 23:34)

In one house it shall be eaten; you shall not carry any of the flesh outside the house, nor shall you break one of its bones. All the congregation of Israel shall keep it. (Exodus 12:46–47)

But when they came to Jesus and saw that He was already dead, they did not break His legs. But one of the soldiers pierced His side with a spear, and immediately blood and water came out. And he who has seen has testified, and his testimony is true; and he knows that he is telling the truth, so that you may believe. For these things were done that the Scripture should be fulfilled, "Not one of His bones shall be broken" And again another Scripture says, "They shall look on Him whom they pierced." (John 19:33–37)

In return for my love they are my accusers, but I give myself to prayer. Thus, they have rewarded me evil for good, and hated for my love. (Psalm 109:4–5)

And those who had laid hold of Jesus led Him away to Caiaphas the high priest, where the scribes and the elders were assembled. But Peter followed Him at a distance to the high priest's courtyard. And he went in and sat with the servants to see the end. Now the chief priests, the elders, and all the council sought false testimony against Jesus to put Him to death, but found none. Even though many false witnesses came forward, they found none. But at last two false witnesses came forward. (Matthew 27:57–60)

But God will redeem my soul from the power of the grave, for He shall receive me. (Psalm 49:15)

And behold, there was a great earthquake; for an angel of the Lord descended from heaven, and came and rolled back the stone from the door, and sat on it. His countenance was like lightning, and his clothing as white as snow.
And the guards shook for fear of him, and became like dead men. But the angel answered and said to the women, "Do not be afraid, for I know that you seek Jesus who was crucified. He is not here; for He is risen, as He said. Come, see the place where the Lord lay. And go quickly and tell His disciples that He is risen from the dead, and indeed He is going before you into Galilee; there you will see Him. Behold, I have told you." (Matthew 28:2–7)

So then, after the Lord had spoken to them, He was received up into heaven, and sat down at the right hand of God. (Mark 16:19)

Lift up your heads, O you gates! And be lifted up, you everlasting doors! And the King of glory shall come in. Who is this King of glory? The Lord strong and mighty, the Lord mighty in battle. Lift up your heads, O you gates! Lift up, you everlasting doors! And the King of glory shall come in. Who is this King of glory? The Lord of hosts, He is the King of glory. (Psalm 24:7–10)

# CHAPTER 11

## SCRIPTURES THAT FEATURE ALL THREE PERSONS OF GOD

Here are scriptures that feature all three Persons of GOD. Remember GOD is three Persons but yet one Holy God.

> Jesus answered him, "The first of all the commandments is: 'Hear, O Israel, the Lord our God, the Lord is one. And you shall love the Lord your God with all your heart, with all your soul, with all your mind, and with all your strength.' This is the first commandment. And the second, like it, is this: 'You shall love your neighbor as yourself.' There is no other commandment greater than these. So the scribe said to Him, "Well said, Teacher. You have spoken the truth, for there is one God, and there is no other but He." (Mark 12:29–32)

> Then God said, "Let Us make man in Our image, according to Our likeness; let them have dominion over the fish of the sea, over the birds of the air, and over the cattle, over all the earth and over every creeping thing that creeps on the earth." So God created man in His own image;

## JESUS IS GOD

in the image of God He created him; male and female created them. (Genesis 1:26–27)

Then the Lord God said, "Behold, the man has become like one of Us, to know good and evil. And now, lest he put out his hand and take also of the tree of life, and eat, and live forever." (Genesis 3:22)

"Come, let Us go down and there confuse their language, that they may not understand one another's speech." So the Lord scattered them abroad from there over the face of all the earth, and they ceased building the city. There its name is called Babel, because there the Lord confused the language of all the earth; and from there the Lord scattered them abroad over the face of all the earth. (Genesis 11:7–9)

Also I heard the voice of the Lord, saying: "Whom shall I send, And who will go for Us?" Then I said, "Here am I! Send me." (Isaiah 6:8)

For unto us a Child is born, unto us a Son is given; And the government will be upon His shoulder. And His name will be called Wonderful, Counselor, Mighty God, Everlasting Father, Prince of Peace. (Isaiah 9:6)

That they may see and know, and consider and understand together, That the hand of the Lord has done this, and the Holy One of Israel has created it. (Isaiah 41:20)

For I am the Lord your God, the Holy One of Israel, your Savior. (Isaiah 43:3a)

"You are My witnesses," says the Lord, "and My servant whom Have chosen, That you may know and believe Me, And understand that I am He. Before Me there was no God formed, Nor shall there be after Me. I, even I, am the Lord, And besides Me there is no savior. I have declared and saved, I have proclaimed, And there was no foreign god among you: Therefore you are My witnesses." Says the Lord, "That I'm God. Indeed before the day was, I'm He; and there is no one who can deliver out of My hand; I work, and who will reverse it?" Thus says the Lord, your Redeemer, the Holy One of Israel: "For your sake I will send to Babylon, And bring them all down as fugitives—the Chaldeans, who rejoiced in their ships." (Isaiah 43:10–16)

"I am the Lord, your Holy One, the Creator of Israel, your King," thus says the Lord, who makes a way in the sea and a path through the mighty waters. (Isaiah 43:10–16)

Thus says the Lord, the King of Israel, and his Redeemer, the Lord of hosts: 'I am the First and I am the Last; besides Me there is no God." (Isaiah 44:6)

Do not fear, nor be afraid; have I not told you from that time, and declared it? You are My witnesses. Is there a God besides Me? Indeed there is no other Rock; I know not one. (Isaiah 44:8)

Thus says the Lord, your Redeemer, and He who formed you from the womb: "I am the Lord, who makes all things, Who stretches out the heavens all alone, Who speaks abroad the earth by Myself." (Isaiah 44:24)

I indeed baptize you with water unto repentance, but He who is coming after me is mightier than I, whose sandals I am not worthy to carry He will baptize you with the Holy Spirit and fire. (Matthew 3:11)

And Jesus came and spoke to them, saying, "All authority has been given to Me in heaven and on earth. Go therefore and make disciples of all the nations, baptizing them in the name of the Father and of the Son and of the Holy Spirit, teaching them to observe all things that I have commanded you; and lo, I am with you always, even to the end of the age," Amen. (Matthew 28:18–20)

"I indeed baptized you with water, but He will baptize you with the Holy Spirit." It came to pass in those days that Jesus came from Nazareth of Galilee, and was baptized by John in the Jordan. And immediately, coming up from the water, He saw the heavens parting and the Spirit descending upon Him like a dove. Then a voice came from heaven, "You are My beloved Son, in whom I am well pleased." (Mark 1:8–11)

When all the people were baptized, it came to pass that Jesus also was baptized; and while He prayed, the heaven was opened. And the Holy Spirit descended in bodily form like a dove upon Him, and a voice came from heaven which said, "You are My beloved Son; in You I am well pleased." (Luke 3:21–22)

And I will pray the Father, and He will give you another Helper, that He may abide with you forever—the Spirit of truth, whom they would cannot receive, because it neither sees Him nor knows Him; but you know Him, for He dwells with you and will be in you. I will not leave you orphans; I will come to you. (John 14:16–18)

But the Helper, the Holy Spirit, whom the Father will send in My name, He will teach you all things, and bring to your remembrance all things that I said to you. (John 14:26)

But when the Helper comes, whom I shall send to you from the Father, the Spirit of Truth who proceeds from the Father, He will testify of Me. (John 15:26)

For the Father Himself loves you, because you have loved Me, and have believed that I came forth from God. I came forth from the Father and have come into the world. Again, I leave the world and go to the Father. (John 16:27–28)

And they were all filled with the Holy Spirit and began to speak with other tongues, as the Spirit gave them utterance. (Acts 2:4)

Therefore being exalted to the right hand of God, and having received from the Father the promise of the Holy Spirit, He poured out this which you now see and hear. (Acts 2:33)

Therefore, take heed to yourselves and to all the flock, among which the Holy Spirit has made you overseers, to shepherd the church of

God which He purchased with His own blood. (Acts 20:28)

Now hope does not disappoint, because the love of God has been poured out in our hearts by the Holy Spirit who was given to us. For when we were still without strength, in due time Christ died for the ungodly. (Romans 5:5–6)

That I might be a minister of Jesus Christ to the Gentiles, ministering the gospel of God, that the offering of the Gentiles might be acceptable, sanctified by the Holy Spirit. Therefore, I have reason to glory in Christ Jesus in the things which pertain to God. (Romans 15:16–17)

The grace of the Lord Jesus Christ, and the love of God, and the communion of the Holy Spirit be with you all. Amen. (2 Corinthians 13:14)

Elect according to the fore knowledge of God the Father, in sanctification of the Spirit, for obedience and sprinkling of the blood of Jesus Christ: Grace to you and peace be multiplied. (1 Peter 1:2)

For there are three that bear witness in heaven: the Father, the Word, and the Holy Spirit; and these three are one. (1 John 5:7)

# CHAPTER 12

## Key Bible Scriptures about Jesus Being God

Genesis 1:1 says, "In the beginning God created the heavens and the earth." In John 1:1–3, it says, "In the beginning was the Word, and the Word was God. He was in the beginning with God. All things were made through Him, and without Him nothing was made that was made."

John 1:14 says, "And the Word became flesh and dwelt among us, and we beheld His glory, the glory as of the only begotten of the Father, full of grace and truth."

After Jesus was resurrected from the dead, I'll pick it up here at John 20:24–29:

> Now Thomas, called the Twin, one of the twelve, was not with them when Jesus came. The other disciples therefore said to him, "We have seen the Lord." So he said to them, "Unless I see in His hands the print of the nails, and put my finger into His side, I will not believe." And after eight days His disciples were again inside, and Thomas with them. Jesus came, the doors being shut, and stood in the midst, and said, "Peace to you!" Then He said to Thomas, "Reach your finger here, and look at My hands; and reach

> your hand here, and put it into My side. Do not be unbelieving, but believing." And Thomas answered and said to Him, "My Lord and my God!" Jesus said to him, "Thomas, because you have seen Me, you have believed. Blessed are those who have not seen and yet have believed."

King David was the king of Israel, reigning from 1010 BC to 970 BC. King David is also known for creating many of the biblical psalms. It is believed that King David lived for seventy years. Jesus was believed to have been born near 4 BC. This means that there may have been just over one thousand years between King David and Jesus. Yet one thousand years before Jesus Christ's birth, King David wrote this in the Psalms:

> For dogs have surrounded Me; the congregation of the wicked has closed Me. They pierced My hands and My feet; I can count all My bones. They look and stare at Me. They divide My garment among them, and for My clothing they cast lots. (Psalm 22:16–18)

What I wanted to point out here is that this is what happened with Jesus just before and being on the cross Matthew 27:35. Please read this in your Bible (NKJV).

> Looking for the blessed hope and glorious appearing of our great God and Savior Jesus Christ, who gave Himself for us, that He might redeem us from every lawless deed and purify for Himself His own special people, zealous for good works. (Titus 2:13–14)

> God who at various times and in various ways spoke in time past to the fathers by the prophets, has in these last days spoken to us

> by His Son, whom He has appointed heir of all things, through whom also He made the worlds; who being the brightness of His glory and the express image of His person, and upholding all things by the word of His power, when He had by Himself purged our sins, sat down at the right hand of the Majesty on high. (Hebrews 1:1–3)

Jesus Christ came down from heaven to earth to redeem us all from sin, because of the fall of Adam and Eve, the first man and woman God created. Since they were the first male and female God created, all of humankind were born from them, since they disobeyed God and fell into sin and spiritual death from God. That is why Jesus came to earth from heaven to sacrifice Himself on a cross for all of mankind's sins so that whosoever would believe on Jesus would be saved.

> Then those who were in the boat came and worshiped Him, saying, "Truly You are the Son of God." (Matthew 14:33)

> And we know that the Son of God has come and has given us an understanding, that we may know Him who is true; and we are in Him who is true, in His Son Jesus Christ. This is the true God and eternal life. (1 John 5:20)

> Nor is there salvation in any other, for there is no other name under heaven given among men by which we must be saved. (Acts 4:12)

> And as they went to tell His disciples, behold, Jesus met them, saying, "Rejoice!" So they came and held Him by the feet and worshiped Him. Then Jesus said to them, "Do not be afraid. God

> and tell My brethren to go to Galilee, and there they will see Me." (Matthew 28:9–10)

In the last scripture, this takes place right after the Sabbath. As the first day of the week began to dawn, Mary Magdalene and the other Mary came to see the tomb. The angel of the Lord showed them were the Lord was and told them to go quickly and tell the disciples.

> Seeing then that we have a great High Priest who has passed through the heavens, Jesus the Son of God, let the heavens Jesus the Son of God, let us hold fast our confession. For we do not have a High Priest who cannot sympathize with our weaknesses, but was in all points tempted as we are, yet without sin. Let us there come boldly to the throne of grace, that we may obtain mercy and find grace to help in time of need. (Hebrews 4:14–16)

> For He made Him who knew no sin to be sin for us, that we might become the righteousness of God in Him. (2 Corinthians 5:21)

> Of whom are the fathers and from whom, according to the flesh, Christ came, who is over all, the eternally blessed God. Amen. (Romans 9:5)

> Has in these last days spoken to us by His Son, whom He has appointed heir of all things, through whom also He made the worlds. (Hebrews 1:2)

> And when they had come into the house, they saw the young Child with Mary, His mother,

and fell down and worshiped Him. And when they had opened their treasures, they presented gifts to Him: gold, frankincense, and myrrh. (Matthew 2:11)

Who Himself bore our sins in His own body on the tree, that we, having died to sins, might live for righteousness—by whose stripes you were healed. (1 Peter 2:24)

And to the angel of the church in Smyrna write, "These things says the First and the last, who was dead, and came to life." (Revelation 2:8)

Jesus heard that they had cast him out; and when He had found him, He said to him, "Do you believe in the Son of God?" He answered and said, "Who is He, Lord, that I may believe in Him?" And Jesus said to him, "You have both seen Him and it is He who is talking with you." Then he said, "Lord I believe!" And he worshiped Him. (John 9:35–38)

To God our Savior, Who alone is wise, be glory and majesty, dominion and power, both now and forever. Amen. (Jude 1:25)

For I have come down from heaven, not to do My own will, but the will of Him who sent Me. (John 6:38)

And Jesus came and spoke to them, saying, "All authority has been given to Me in heaven and on earth." (Matthew 28:18)

# JESUS IS GOD

> Men of Israel, hear these words: Jesus of Nazareth, a Man attested by God to you by miracles, wonders, and signs which God did through Him in your midst, as you yourselves also know—Him, being delivered by the determined purpose and foreknowledge of God, you have taken by lawless hands, have crucified, and put to death; whom God raised up having loosed the pains of death, because it was not possible that He should be held by it. (Acts 2:22)

Jesus, who is God the Son, came to earth from heaven and lived a sinless life. He is also known as the second Adam.

> And so it is written, "The first man Adam became a living being. The last Adam became a life-giving spirit. However, the spiritual is not first, but the natural, and afterward the spiritual. The first man was of the earth, made of dust; the second Man is the Lord from heaven. He was falsely accused beaten, whipped, spat on, punched, beard ripped out, mocked, and crucified, pierced with nail spikes in His hands and in His feet, also speared in His side. He did it all for the Love of All nations and people, that whosoever will repent of their sins and follow Jesus will be saved." (1 Corinthians 15:45–47)

These are some of the signs, wonders, and miracles mentioned in Acts.

> Jesus said to them, "Fill the waterspouts with water." And they filled them up to the brim. And He said to them, "Draw some out now, and take it to the master of the feast." And they took it. When the master of the feast had tested the water

that was made wine, and did not know where it came from (but the servants who had drawn the water knew), the master of the feast called the bridegroom. And he said to him, "Every man at the beginning sets out the good wine, and when the guests have well drunk, then the inferior. You have kept the good wine until now!" This beginning of signs Jesus did in Cana of Galilee, and manifested His glory; and His disciples believed in Him. (John 2:7–11)

So Jesus came again to Cana of Galilee where He had made the water wine. And there was a certain nobleman whose son was sick at Capernaum. When he heard that Jesus had come out of Judea into Galilee, he went to Him and implored Him to come down and heal his son, for he was at the point of death. Then Jesus said to Him, "Unless you people see signs and wonders, you will by no means believe." The nobleman said to Him, "Sir, come down before my child dies!" Jesus said to him, "Go your way; your son lives." So the man believed the word that Jesus spoke to him, and he went his way. And as he was now going down, his servants met him and told him, saying, "Your son lives!" Then he inquired of them the hour when he got better. And they said to him, "Yesterday at the seventh hour the fever left him." So the father knew that it was at the same hour in which Jesus said to him, "Your son lives." And he himself believed, and his whole household. This again is the second sign Jesus did when He had come out of Judea into Galilee. (John 4:46–54)

Now there is in Jerusalem by the Sheep Gate a pool, which is called in Hebrew, Bethesda, having five porches. In these lay a great multitude of sick people, blind, lame, paralyzed, waiting for the moving of the water. For an angel went down at a certain time into the pool and stirred up the water; then whoever stepped in first, after the stirring of the water, was made well of whatever disease he had. Now a certain man was there who had an infirmity thirty-eight years. When Jesus saw him lying there and knew that he already had been in that condition a long time, He said to him, "Do you want to be made well?" The sick man answered Him, "Sir, I have no man to put me into the pool when the water is stirred; but while I am coming, another steps down before me." Jesus said to him, "Rise, take up your bed and walk." And immediately the man was made well, took up his bed, and walked. And that day was the Sabbath. The Jews therefore said to him who was cured, "It is the Sabbath; it is not lawful for you to carry your bed." He answered them, "He who made me well said to me, 'Take up your bed and walk.'" (John 5:2–9)

After these things Jesus went over the Sea of Galilee, which is the Sea of Tiberius. Then a great multitude followed Him, because they saw His signs which He performed on those who were diseased. And Jesus went up on the mountain, and there He sat with His disciples. Now the Passover, a feast of the Jews, was near. Then Jesus lifted up His eyes, and seeing a great multitude coming toward Him, He said to Philip, "Where shall we buy bread, that these may eat?" But this He said to test him, for He Himself knew

> what He would do. Philip answered Him, "Two hundred denarii worth of bread is not sufficient for them, that every one of them may have a little." One of His disciples, Andrew, Simon Peter's brother, said to Him, "There is a lad here who has five barley loaves and two small fish, but what are they among so many?" Then Jesus said, "Make the people sit down," Now there was much grass in the place. So the men sat down, in number about five thousand. And Jesus took the loaves, and when He had given thanks He distributed them to the disciples, and the disciples to those sitting down; and likewise of the fish, as much as they wanted. So when they were filled, He said to His disciples, "Gather up the fragments that remain, so that nothing is lost." Therefore they gather them up, and filled twelve baskets with the fragments of the five barley loaves which were left over by those who had eaten. Then those men, when they had seen the sign that Jesus did, said, "This is truly the Prophet who is to come into the world." (John 6:1–14)

The people didn't fully understand that Jesus is fully God sent from heaven.

> Immediately, Jesus made His disciples get into the boat and go before Him to the other side, while He sent the multitudes away. And when He had sent the multitudes away, He went up on the mountain by Himself to pray. Now when evening came, He was alone there. But the boat was now I the middle of the sea, tossed by the waves, for the wind was contrary, now in the fourth watched of the night Jesus went to them, walking on the sea. And when the disciples saw

Him walking on the sea, they were troubled, saying, "It is a ghost!" And they cried out for fear. But immediately Jesus spoke to them, saying, "Be of good cheer! It is I; do not be afraid." And Peter answered Him and said, "Lord, if it is You, command me to come to You on the water." So He said, "Come." And when Peter had come down out of the boat, he walked on the water to go to Jesus. But when he saw that the wind was boisterous, he was afraid; and beginning to sink he cried out, saying "Lord, save me!"

And immediately Jesus stretched out His hand and caught him, and said to him, "O you of little faith, why did you doubt?" And when they got into the boat, the wind ceased. Then those who were in the boat came and worshiped Him, saying, "Truly You are the Son of God." (Matthew 14:22–33)

Now as Jesus passed by, He saw a man who was blind from birth. And His disciples asked Him, saying, "Rabbi, who sinned, this man or his parents, that he was born blind?" Jesus answered, "Neither this man nor his parents sinned, but that the works of God should be revealed in him. "I must work the works of Him who sent Me while it is day; the night is coming when no one can work. "As long as I am in the world, I am the light of the world." When He had said these things, He spat on the ground and made clay with the saliva; and He anointed the eyes of the blind man with the clay. And He said to Him, "Go, wash in the pool of Siloam" (which is translated, Sent). Do he went and washed, and came back seeing. Therefore the neighbors and those who previously had seen that he was blind said, "Is not this he who sat and begged?" Some said, "This is he." Others said, "He is like him." He said, "I am he." Therefore they said to him, "How were your eyes opened?" He answered and said, "A Man called Jesus made clay and anointed my eyes and said to me, 'Go to the pool of Siloam and wash.' So I went and washed, and I received sight." (John 9:1–11)

Now a certain man was sick, Lazarus of Bethany, the town of Mary and her sister Martha. It was that Mary who anointed the Lord with fragrant oil and wiped His feet with her hair, whose brother Lazarus was sick. Therefore, the sister sent to Him, saying, 'Lord, behold, he whom You love is sick." When Jesus heard that, He said, "This sickness is not unto death, but for the glory of God, that the Son of God may be glorified through it." Now Jesus loved Martha and her sister and Lazarus. So, when He heard that he was sick, He stayed two more days in the place where He was. Then after this He said to the disciples, "Let us go to Judea again." The disciples said to Him, "Rabbi, lately the Jews sought to stone You, and are You going there again?" Jesus answered, "Are there not twelve hours in the day? If anyone walks in the day, he does not stumble, because he sees the light of this world. "But if one walks in the night, he stumbles, because the light is not in him." These things He said, and after that He said to them, "Our friend Lazarus sleeps, but I go that I may wake him up." Then His disciples said, "Lord, if he sleeps he will get well." However, Jesus spoke of his death, but they thought that He was speaking about taking rest in sleep. Then Jesus said to them plainly, "Lazarus is dead. And

# JESUS IS GOD

I am glad for your sakes that I was not there, that you may believe, Nevertheless let us go to him." Then Thomas, who is called the Twin, said to his fellow disciples, "Let us also go, that we may die with Him."

So when Jesus came, He found that he had already been in the tomb four days. Now Bethany was near Jerusalem, about two mile away. And many of the Jews had joined the women around Martha and Mary, to comfort them concerning their brother. Then Martha, as soon as she heard that Jesus was coming, went and met Him, but Mary was sitting in the house. Now Martha said to Jesus, "Lord, if You had been here, my brother would not have died. But even now I know that whatever You ask of God, God will give You." Jesus said to her, "Your brother will rise again." Martha said to Him, "Know that he will rise again in the resurrection at the last day." Jesus said to her, "I am the resurrection and the life. He who believes in Me, though he may die, de shall live. And whoever lives and believes in Me shall never die. Do you believe this?" She said to Him, "Yes, Lord, I believe that You are the Christ, the Son of God, who is to come into the world." And when she had said these things, she went her way and secretly called Mary her sister, saying, "The Teacher has come and is calling for you." As soon as she heard that, she arose quickly and came to Him. Now Jesus had not yet come into the town, but was in the place where Martha met Him. Then the Jews who were with her in the house, and comforting her, when they saw that Mary rose up quickly and went out, followed her, saying, "She is going to the tomb to weep there."

Then, when Mary came where Jesus was, and saw Him, she fell down at His feet, saying to Him, "Lord, if You had been here, my brother would not have died," Therefore, when Jesus saw her weeping, and the Jews who came with her weeping, He groaned in the spirit and was troubled. And He said, "Where have you laid him?" They said to Him, "Lord, come and see." Jesus wept. Then the Jews said, "See how He loved him!" And some of them said, "Could not this Man, who opened the eyes the blind, also have kept this man from dying?" Then Jesus, again groaning in Himself, came to the tomb. It was a cave, and a stone lay against it. Jesus said, "Take away the stone." Martha, the sister of him who was dead, said to Him, "Lord, by this time there is a stench, for he has been dead four days." Jesus said to her, "Did I not say to you that if you would believe you would see the glory of God?" Then they took away the stone from the place where the dead man was lying. And Jesus lifted up His eyes and said, "Father, I thank You that You have heard Me. And I know that You always hear Me, but because of the people who are standing by I said this, that they may believe that You sent Me." Now when He had said these things, He cried with a loud voice, "Lazarus, come forth!" And he who had died came out bound hand and foot with grave clothes, and his face was wrapped with a cloth. Jesus said to them "Loose him, and let him go." Then many of the Jews who had come to Mary and had seen the things Jesus did believed in Him. (John 11:1–45)

# CHAPTER 13

## Why Is Jesus So Important and Vital for Every Nation and All People

1) Because He is our Creator. He made us all. Genesis 1:26–27 says, "Then God said, 'Let Us make man in Our image, according to Our likeness; let them have dominion over the fish of the sea, over the birds of the air, and over the cattle, over all the earth and over every creeping thing that creep on the earth.' So God created man in His own image; in the image of God He created them."
2) Jesus loved us first while we were yet in our sins. First John 4:19–21 says, "We love Him because He first loved us. If someone says, 'I love God,' and hates his brother, he is a liar; for he who does not love his brother whom he has seen, how can he love God whom he has not seen? And this commandment we have from Him: that he who loves God must love his brother also."
3) We all have the ability to exercise our free will; however, God explains what is best. Deuteronomy 30:19–20 says, "I call heaven and earth as witnesses to day against you, that I have set before you life and death, blessing and cursing; therefore, choose life, that both you and your descendants may live; that you may love the Lord your God, that you may obey His voice, and that you may cling to Him, for He is your life and the length of your days; and that you may dwelling the land which the Lord swore to your fathers, to Abraham, Isaac, and Jacob, to give them!"

4) Jesus loves us all, and gives us all new opportunities to follow Him. Lamentations 3:22–23 says, "Through the Lord's mercies we are not consumed, Because His compassions fail not. They are new every morning; Great is Your faithfulness."
5) It is because of Jesus's goodness that leads us to Him. Romans 2:4 says, "Or do you despise the riches of His goodness, forbearance, and long-suffering, not knowing that the goodness of God leads you to repentance?"

However, there is a consequence if you choose not to have Jesus as Lord.

> But to those who are self-seeking and do not obey the truth, but obey unrighteousness-indignation and wrath, tribulation and anguish, on every soul of man who does evil, of the Jew first and also of the Greek; but glory, honor, and peace to everyone who works what is good, to the Jew first and also to the Greek. For there is no partiality with God. (Romans 2:8–11)

> For God so loved the world that He gave His only begotten Son, that whoever believes in Him should not perish but have everlasting life. For God did not send His Son into the world to condemn the world, but that the world through Him might be saved. He who believes in Him is not condemned; but he who does not believe is condemned already, because he has not believed in the name of the only begotten Son of God. And this is the condemnation, that the light has come into the world, and men loved darkness rather than light, because their deeds were evil. For everyone practicing evil hates the light and does not come to the light, lest his deeds should be exposed. But he who does the truth comes to

## JESUS IS GOD

> the light, that his deeds may be clearly seen, that they have been done in God. (John 3:16–21)

Jesus conquered death, hell, and the grave for us. Meaning, whosoever will believe in Jesus Christ as their personal Lord and Savior shall be saved. Romans 10:13 says, "For whoever calls on the name of the Lord shall be saved."

Now here's what the Bible says about this subject:

> And do not fear those who kill the body but cannot kill the soul. But rather fear Him who is able to destroy both soul and body in hell. (Matthew 10:28)

> I am He who lives, and was dead, and behold, I am alive forevermore. Amen. And I have the keys of Hades and of Death. (Revelation 1:18)

> Then He will also say to those on the left hand, "Depart from Me, you cursed, into the everlasting fire prepared for the devil and his angels." (Matthew 25:41)

> But the cowardly, unbelieving, abominable, murders, sexually immoral, sorcerers, idolaters, and all liars shall have their part in the lake which burns with fire and brimstone, which is the second death. (Revelation 21:8)

> For You will not leave my soul in Hades, nor will You allow Your Holy One to see corruption. (Acts 2:27)

> And these will go away into everlasting punishment but the righteous into eternal life. (Matthew 25:46)

For the wages of sin is death, but the gift of God is eternal life in Christ Jesus our Lord. (Romans 6:23)

He foreseeing this, spoke concerning the resurrection of the Christ, that His soul was not left in Hades, nor did His flesh see corruption. This Jesus God has raised up, of which we are all witnesses. (Acts 2:31–32)

If your hand causes you to sin, cut it off. It is better for you to enter into life maimed, rather than having two hands, to go to hell, into the fire that shall never be quenched—where "their worm does not die, and the fire is not quenched." And if your foot causes you to sin, cut it off. It is better of you to enter life lame, rather than having two feet, to be cast into hell, into the fire that shall never be quenched—where "Their worm does not die, And the fire is not quenched." And if your eyes cause you to sin, pluck it out. It is better for you to enter the kingdom of God with one eye, rather than having two eyes, to be cast into hell fire—where "their worm does not die, And the fire is not quenched." For everyone will be seasoned with fire, and every sacrifice will be seasoned with salt. Salt is good, but if the salt loses its flavor, how will you season it? Have salt in yourselves, and have peace with one another. (Mark 9:43–50)

The sea gave up the dead who were in it, and Death and Hades delivered up the dead who were in them. And they were judged, each one according to his works. Then Death and Hades were cast into the lake of fire. This is the second death. (Revelation 20:13–14)

I will ransom them from the power of the grave; I will redeem them from death. O Death, I will be you plagues! O Grave, will be your destruction! Pity is hidden from My eyes. (Hosea 13:14)

Inasmuch then as the children have partaken of flesh and blood, He Himself likewise shared in the same, that through death He might destroy him who had the power of death, that is the devil, and release those who through fear of death were all their lifetime subject to bondage. For indeed He does not give aid to angels, but He does give aid to the seed of Abraham. Therefore, in all things He had to be made like His brethren, that He might be a merciful and faithful High Priest in things pertaining to God, to make propitiation for the sins of the people. For in that He Himself has suffered, being temped, He is able to aid those who are tempted. (Hebrews 2:14–18)

He then would have had to suffer often since the foundation of the world; but now, once at the end of the ages, He has appeared to put away sin by the sacrifice of Himself. And as it is appointed of men to die once, but after this the judgment so Christ was offered once to bear the sins of many. To those who eagerly wait for Him He will appear a second time, apart from sin, for salvation. (Hebrews 9:26–28)

As Sodom and Gomorrah, and the cities around them in a similar manner to these, having given themselves over to sexual immorality and gone after strange flesh, are set forth as an example, suffering the vengeance of eternal fire. (Jude 1:7)

And God will wipe away every tear from their eyes; there shall be no more death, nor sorrow, nor crying. There shall be no more pain, for the former things have passed away. (Revelation 21:4)

Which is manifest evidence of the righteous judgment of God, that you may be counted worthy of the kingdom of God, for which you also suffer; since it is a righteous thing with God to repay with tribulation those who trouble you, and to give you who are troubled rest with us when the Lord Jesus is revealed from heaven with His mighty angels, in flaming fire taking vengeance on those who do not know God, and on those who do not obey the gospel of our Lord Jesus Christ. These shall be punished with everlasting destruction from the presence of the Lord and from the glory of His power, when He comes, in that Day, to be glorified in His saints and to be admired among all those who believe, because our testimony among you was believed. Therefore, we also pray always for you that our God would count you worthy of this calling, and fulfill all the good pleasure of His goodness and the work of faith with power, that the name of the Lord Jesus Christ may be glorified in you, and you in Him, according to the grace of our God and the Lord Jesus Christ. (2 Thessalonians 1:5–12)

For if God did not spare the angels who sinned, but cast them down to hell and delivered them into chains of darkness, to be reserved for judgment; and did not spare the ancient world, but saved Noah, one of the eight people, a preacher righteousness, bringing in the flood on the world of the ungodly; and turning the cities of Sodom and Gomorrah into ashes, condemned them to destruction, making them an example to those who afterward would live ungodly; and delivered righteous Lot, who was oppressed by the filthy conduct of the wicked (for that righteous man, dwelling among them, tormented his righteous soul from day to day by seeing and hearing their lawless deeds)—then the Lord knows how to deliver godly out of temptations and to reserve the unjust under punishment for the day of judgment, and especially those who walk according to the flesh in the lust of uncleanness and despise authority. They are presumptuous, self-willed. They are not afraid to speak evil of dignitaries. (2 Peter 2:4–9)

There was a certain rich man who was clothed in purple and fine linen and fared sumptuously every day. But there was a certain beggar named Lazarus, full of sores, who was laid at his gate, desiring to be fed with the crumbs which fell from the rich man's table. Moreover, the dogs came and licked his sores. So it was that the beggar died, and was carried by the angels to Abraham's bosom. The rich man also died and was buried. And being in torments in Hades, he lifted up his eyes and saw Abraham afar off, and Lazarus in his bosom. Then he cried and said, "Father Abraham, have mercy on me, and send

Lazarus that he may dip the tip of his finger in water and cool my tongue; for I am tormented in this flame." But Abraham said, "Son, remember that in your lifetime you received your good things, and likewise Lazarus evil things; but now he is comforted and you are tormented. And besides all this, between us and you there is great gulf fixed, so that those who want to pass from here to you cannot, nor can those from there pass to us." Then he said, "I beg you therefore, father, that you would send him to my father's house, for I have five brothers, that he may testify to them, lest they also come to this place of torment." Abraham said to him, "They have Moses and the prophets; let them hear them." And he said, "No, father Abraham; but if one goes to them from the dead, they will repent." But he said to him, "If they do not hear Moses and the prophets, neither will they be persuaded though one rise from the dead." (Luke 16:19–31)

Then he said to Jesus, "Lord, remember me when You come into Your kingdom." And Jesus said to him, "Assuredly, I say to you, today you will be with Me in Paradise." (Luke 23:42–43)

For it is better, if it is the will of God, to suffer for doing good than for doing evil. For Christ also suffered once for sins, the just for the unjust, that He might bring us to God, being put to death in the flesh but made alive by the Spirit, by whom also He went and preached to the spirits in prison, who formerly were disobedient, when once the Divine long-suffering waited in the days of Noah, while the ark was being prepared, in which a few, that is, eight souls, were saved through water. There is also an antitype which now saves us—baptism (not the removal of the filth of the flesh, but the answer of a good conscience toward God), through the resurrection of Jesus Christ, who has gone into heaven and is at the right hand of God, angels and authorities and powers having been made subject to Him. (1 Peter 3:17–22)

The first man was of the earth, made of dust; the second Man is the Lord from heaven. As was the man of dust, so also are those who are made of dust; and as is the heavenly Man, so also are those who are heavenly. And as we have borne the image of the man of dust, we shall also bear the image of the heavenly Man. Now this I say, brethren, that flesh and blood cannot inherit the kingdom of God; nor does corruption inherit incorruption. Behold, I tell you a mystery; We shall not all sleep, but we shall all be changed—in a moment, in the twinkling of an eye, at the last trumpet. For the trumpet will sound, and the dead will be raised incorruptible, and we shall be changed. For this corruptible must put on incorruption, and this mortal must put on immortality. So when this corruption has put on incorruption, and this mortal has put on immortality, then shall be brought to pass the saying that is written: "Death is swallowed up in victory. O Death, where is your sting? O Hades, where is your victory?" The sting of death is sin, and the strength of sin is the law. But thanks be to God, who gives us the victory through our Lord Jesus Christ. (1 Corinthians 15:47–57)

The devil, who deceived them, was cast into the lake of fire and brimstone where the beast and the false prophet are, And they will be tormented day and night forever and ever. (Revelation 20:10)

Then the dust will return to the earth as it was, And the spirit will return to God who gave it. (Ecclesiastes 12:7)

Then the beast was captured, and with him the false prophet who worked signs in his presence, by which he deceived those who received the mark of the beast and those who worshiped his image. These two were cast alive into the lake of fire during with brimstone. (Revelation 19:20)

They will give an account to Him who is ready to judge the living and the dead. For this reason the gospel was preached also to those who are dead, that they might be judged according to men in the flesh, but live according to God in the spirit. But the end of all things is at hand; therefore be serious and watchful in your prayers. And above all things have fervent love for one another, for "love will cover a multitude of sins." Be hospitable to one another without grumbling. As each one has received a gift, minister it to one another, as good stewards of the manifold grace of God. (1 Peter 4:5–10)

Again, the kingdom of heaven is like a dragnet that was cast into the sea and gathered some of every kind, which, when it was full, they drew to shore; and they sat down and gathered the good into vessels, but threw the bad away. So it will be

## JESUS IS GOD

at the end of the age. The angels will come forth, separate the wicked from among the just, and cast them into the furnace of fire. There will be wailing and gnashing of teeth. Jesus sad to them, "Have you understood all these things?" They said to Him, "Yes, Lord." (Matthew 13:47–51)

But has now been revealed by the appearing of our Savior Jesus Christ, who has abolished death and brought life and immortality to light through the gospel. (2 Timothy 1:10)

Therefore, if anyone is in Christ, he is a new creation; old things have passed away; behold, all things have become new. Now all things are of God, who has reconciled us to Himself through Jesus Christ, and has given us the ministry of reconciliation, that is, that God was in Christ reconciling the world to Himself, not imputing their trespasses to them, and has committed to us the word of reconciliation. Now then, we are ambassadors for Christ, as though God were pleading through us: we implore you on Christ's behalf, be reconciled to God. For He made Him who knew no sin to be sin for us, that we might become the righteousness of God in Him. (2 Corinthians 5:17–21)

Who Himself bore our sins in His own body on the tree, that we, having died to sins, might live for righteousness—by whose strips you were healed. For you were like sheep going astray, but have now returned to the Shepard and Overseer of your souls. (1 Peter 2:24–25)

The last enemy that will be destroyed is death. (1 Corinthians 15:26)

Blessed and holy is he who has part in the first resurrection. Over such the second death has no power, but they shall be priests of God and of Christ, and shall reign with Him a thousand years. (Revelation 20:6)

Having disarmed principalities and powers, He made a public spectacle of them, triumphing over them in it. (Colossians 2:15)

But God demonstrates His own love towards us, in that while we were still sinners, Christ died for us. Much more then, having now been justified by His blood, we shall be saved from wrath through Him. For if when we were enemies we were reconciled to God through the death of His Son, much more, having been reconciled, we shall be saved by His life. And not only that, but we also rejoice in God through our Lord Jesus Christ, through whom we have now received the reconciliation. Therefore, just as through one man sin entered the world, and death through sin, and thus death speak to all men, because all sinned. (Romans 5:8–12)

We are confident, yes, well pleased rather to be absent from the body and to be present with the Lord. (2 Corinthians 5:8)

Jesus said to her, "I am the resurrection and the life. He who believes in Me though he may die, he shall live. And whoever lives and believes in Me shall never die. Do you believe this?" (John 11:25–26)

He said to them, "But who do you say that I am?" Simon Peter answered and said, "You are the Christ, the Son of the living God." Jesus answered and said to him, "Blessed are you, Simon Bar-Jonah, for flesh and blood has not revealed this to you, but My Father who is in heaven. And I also say to you that you are Peter, and on this rock I will build My church, and the gates of Hades shall not prevail against it. And I will give you the keys of the kingdom of heaven, and whatever you bind on earth will be bound in heaven, and whatever you loose on earth will be loosed in heaven." (Matthew 16:15–19)

He will swallow up death forever, and the Lord God will wipe away tears from all faces; the rebuke of His people He will take away from all the earth; for the Lord has spoken. And it will be said in that day: "Behold, this is our God; We have waited for Him, and He will save us. This is the Lord; we have waited for Him; we will be glad and rejoice in His salvation." (Isaiah 25:8–9)

And anyone not found written in the Book of Life was cast into the lake of fire. (Revelation 20:15)

But now the righteousness of God apart from the law is revealed, being witnessed by the Law and the Prophets, even the righteousness of God, through faith in Jesus Christ, to all and on all who believe. For there is no difference; for all have sinned and fall short of the glory of

God, being justified freely by His grace through the redemption that in Christ Jesus. (Romans 3:21–24)

For You will not leave my soul in Sheol, nor will You allow Your Holy One to see corruption. You will show me the path of life; in Your presence is fullness of joy; At Your right hand are pleasures forevermore. (Psalm 16:10–11)

Now this, "He ascended"—what does it mean but that He also first descended into the lower parts of the earth? He who descended is also the One who ascended far above all the heavens, that He might fill all things. (Ephesians 4:9–10)

Most assuredly, I say to you, he who hears My word and believes in Him who sent Me has everlasting life, and shall not come into judgment, but has passed from death into life. (John 5:24)

Men of Israel, hear these words: Jesus of Nazareth, a Man attested by God to you by miracles, wonders and signs which God did through Him in your midst, as you yourselves also know—Him, being delivered by the determined purpose and foreknowledge of God, you have taken by lawless hands, have crucified, and put to death; whom God raised up, having loosed the pains of death, because it was not possible that He should be held by it. (Acts 2:22–24)

Do not marvel at this; for the hour is coming in which all who are in graves will hear His voice and come forth—those who have done good, to the resurrection of life, and those who have done evil, to the resurrection of condemnation. I can of Myself do nothing. As I hear, I judge; and My judgment is righteous, because I do not seek My own will but the will of the Father who sent Me. (John 5:28–30)

And war broke out in heaven: Michael and his angels fought with the dragon; and the dragon and his angels fought, but they did not prevail, nor was a place found for them in heaven any longer. So the great dragon was cast out, that serpent of old, called the Devil and Satin, who deceives the whole world; he was cast to the earth, and his angels were cast out with him. Then I heard a loud voice saying in heaven, "Now salvation, and strength, and the kingdom of our God, and the power of His Christ have come, for the accuser of our brethren, who accused them before our God day and night, has been cast down. and they overcame him by the blood of the lamb and by the word of their testimony, and they did not love their lives to death. Therefore rejoice, O heavens, and you who dwell in them! Woe to the inhabitants of the earth and the sea! For the devil has come down to you, having great wrath, because he knows that he has a short time." (Revelation 12:7–12)

And I will give you the keys of the kingdom of heaven, and whatever you bind on earth will be bound in heaven, and whatever you loose on earth will be loosed in heaven. (Matthew 16:19)

And He is the head of the body, the church, who is the beginning, the first born from the dead, that in all things He may have the preeminence. For it pleased the Father that in Him all the fullness should dwell, and by Him to reconcile all things to Himself, by Him, whether things on earth or things in heaven, having made peace through the blood of His cross. And you, who once were alienated and enemies in your mind by wicked works, yet now He has reconciled in the body of His flesh through death, to present you holy, and blameless, and above reproach in His sight. (Colossians 1:18–22)

But we see Jesus, who was made a little lower than Elohim, for the suffering of death crowned with glory and honor, that He, by the graces of God, might taste death for everyone. (Hebrews 2:9)

If we say that we have fellowship with Him, and walk in darkness, we lie and do not practice the truth. But if we walk in the light as He is in the light, we have fellowship with one another, and the blood of Jesus Christ His Son cleanses us from all sin. If we say that we have no sin, we deceive ourselves, and the truth is not in us. If we confess our sins, He is faithful and just to forgive us our sins and to cleanse us from all unrighteousness. If we say that we have not sinned, we make Him a liar, and His word is not in us. (1 John 1:6–10)

But I do not want you to be ignorant, brethren, concerning those who have fallen asleep, lest you sorrow as others who have no hope. For if we believe that Jesus died and rose again, even so God will bring with Him those who sleep in Jesus. For this we say to you by the word of the Lord, that we who are alive and remain until the coming of the Lord will by no means precede those who are asleep. For the Lord Himself will descend from heaven with a shout, with the voice of an archangel, and with the trumpet of God. And the dead in Christ will rise first. Then we who are alive and remain shall be caught up to gather with them in the clouds to meet the lord in the air. And thus we shall always be with the Lord. Therefore, comfort one another with these words. (1 Thessalonians 4:13–18)

For God has not given us a spirit of fear, but of power and love and of a sound mind. (2 Timothy 1:7)

Or do you not know that as many of us as were baptized into Christ Jesus were baptized into His death? Therefore, we were buried with Him through baptism into death, that just as Christ was raised from the dead by the glory of the Father, even so we also should walk in newness of life. (Romans 6:3–4)

Rejoice in the Lord always. Again I say, rejoice! Let your gentleness be known to all men. The Lord is at hand. Be anxious of nothing, but in everything by prayer and supplication, with thanksgiving, let your request be made known to God: and the peace of God, which surpasses all understanding, will guard your hearts and minds through Christ Jesus. Finally, brethren, whatever things are true, whatever things are noble, whatever things are just, whatever things are pure, whatever things are lovely, whatever things are of good report, if there is any virtue and if there is anything praiseworthy—meditate on these things. (Philippians 4:4–8)

And many of those who sleep in the dust of the earth shall awake, Some to everlasting life, some to shame and everlasting contempt. (Daniel 12:2)

The Father loves the Son, and has given all things into His hand. He who believes in the Son has everlasting life; and he who does not believe the Son shall not see life, but the wrath of God abides on him. (John 3:35–36)

Blessed be the God and Father of our Lord Jesus Christ, who according to His abundant mercy has begotten us again to a living hope through the resurrection of Jesus Christ from the dead, to an inheritance incorruptible and undefiled and that does not fade away, reserved in heaven for you, who are kept by the power of God through faith for salvation ready to be revealed in the last time. (1 Peter 1:3–5)

One Lord, one faith, one baptism, one God and Father of all, who is above all, and through all, and in you all. But to each one of us grace was given according to the measure of Christ's gift. Therefore, He says, "When He ascended on high, He led captivity captive, And gave gifts to men." (Ephesians 4:5–8)

## JESUS IS GOD

> But now Christ is risen from the dead, and has become the first fruits of those who have fallen asleep. For since by man came death, by Man also came the resurrection of the dead. For as in Adam all die, even so in Christ all shall be made alive. (1 Corinthians 15:20–22)

> But He answered and said to them, "An evil and adulterous generation seeks after a sign, and no sign will be given to it except the sign of the prophet Jonah. For as Jonah was three days and three nights in the belly of the great fish, so will the Son of Man be three days and three nights in the heart of the earth. The men of Nineveh will rise up in the judgment with this generation and condemn it, because they repented at the preaching of Jonah; and indeed a greater than Jonah is here. (Matthew 12:39–41)

# CHAPTER 14

## Scriptures on Salvation

That if you confess with your mouth the Lord Jesus and believe in your heart that God has raised Him from the dead, you will be saved. For with the heart one believes unto righteousness, and with the mouth confession is made unto salvation. For the Scripture says, "Whoever believes on Him will not be put to shame." For there is no distinction between Jew and Greek, for the same Lord over all is rich to all who call upon Him. For "whoever calls on the name of the Lord shall be saved." (Romans 10:9–13)

This is the "stone which was rejected by you builders, which has become the chief cornerstone." Nor is there salvation in any other, for there is no other name under heaven given among men by which we must be saved. (Acts 4:11–12)

And he brought them out and said, "Sir, what must I do to be saved?" So they said, "Believe on the Lord Jesus Christ, and you will be saved, you and your household." (Acts 16:30–31)

# JESUS IS GOD

Therefore, do not be ashamed of the testimony of our Lord, nor of me His prisoner, but share with in the sufferings for the gospel according to the power of God, who has saved us and called us with a holy calling, not according to our works, but according to His own purpose and grace which was given to us in Christ Jesus before time began, but has now been revealed by the appearing of our Savior Jesus Christ, who has abolished death and brought life and immortality to light through the gospel. (2 Timothy 1:8–10)

Truly my soul silently waits for God; from Him comes my salvation. He only is my rock and my salvation; He is my defense; I shall not be greatly moved. (Psalm 62:1–2)

The sun shall be turned into darkness, and the moon into blood, before the coming of the great and awesome day of the Lord. And it shall come to pass that whoever calls on the name of the Lord shall be saved. (Acts 2:20–21)

Do you not know that the unrighteous will not inherit the kingdom of God? Do not be deceived. Neither fornicators, nor idolaters, nor adulterers, nor homosexuals, nor sodomites, nor thieves, nor covetous, nor drunkards, nor revilers, nor extortioners will inherit the kingdom of God. And such were some of you. But you were washed, but you were sanctified, but you were justified in the name of the Lord Jesus and by the Spirit of our God. (1 Corinthians 6:9–11)

For the grace of God that brings salvation has appeared to all men, teaching us that, denying ungodliness and worldly lusts, we should live soberly, righteously, and godly in the present age, looking for the blessed hope and glorious appearing of our great God and Savior Jesus Christ, who gave Himself focus, that He might redeem us from every lawless deed and purify for Himself His own special people, zealous for good works. (Titus 2:11–14)

And Jesus said to him, "Today salvation has come to this house, be because he also is a son of Abraham; for the Son of Man has come to seek and to save that which was lost." (Luke 19:9–10)

But, beloved, do not forget this one thing, that with the Lord one day is as a thousand years, and a thousand years as one day. The Lord is not slack concerning His promise, as some count slackness but is long-suffering toward us, not willing that any should perish but that all should come to repentance. But the day of the Lord will come as a thief in the night, in which the heavens will pass away with a great noise, and the elements will melt with fervent heat; both the earth and the works that are in it will be burned up. Therefore, since all these things will be dissolved, what manner of persons ought you to be in holy conduct and godliness, looking for and hastening the coming of the day of God, because of which the heavens will be dissolved, being on fire, and the elements will melt with fervent heat? (2 Peter 3:8–12)

Enter by the narrow gate; for wide is the gate and broad is the way that leads to destruction, and there are many who go in by it. Because narrow is the gate and difficult is the way which leads to life, and there are few who find it. (Matthew 7:13–14)

And He said to them, "Go into all the world and preach the gospel to every creature. He who believes and is baptized will be saved; but he who does not believe will be condemned. (Mark 16:15–16)

Who are kept by the power of God through faith for salvation ready to be revealed in the last time. (1 Peter 1:5)

Whom having not seen you love though now you do not see Him, yet believing, you rejoice with joy inexpressible and full of glory, receiving the end of your faith—the salvation of your souls. (1 Peter 1:8–9)

For I am the least of the apostles, who am not worthy to be called an apostle, because I persecuted the church of God. But by the grace of God I am what I am, and His grace toward me was not in vain; but I labor more abundantly than they all, yet not I but the grace of God which was with me. There, whether it was I or they, so we preach and so you believed. Now if Christ is preached that He has been raised from the dead, how do some among you say that there is no resurrection of the dead? But if there is no resurrection of the dead, then Christ is not risen. And Christ is not risen, then our preaching is empty and your faith is also empty. Yes, and we are found false witnesses of God, because we have testified of God that He raised up Christ, whom He did not raise up—if in fact the dead do not rise. For if the dead do not rise, then Christ is not risen. And if Christ is not risen, your faiths futile; you are still in your sins! Then also those who have fallen asleep in Christ have perished. If in this life only we have hope in Christ, we are of all men the most pitiable. But now Christ is risen from the dead, and has become the first fruits of those who have fallen asleep. For since by man came death, by Man also came the resurrection of the dead. For as in Adam all die, even so in Christ all shall be made alive. But each one in his own order; Christ the first fruits, afterward those who are Christ's at His coming. Then comes the end, when He delivers the kingdom to God the Father, when He puts an end to all rule and all authority and power. For He must reign till He has put all enemies under His feet. The last enemy that will be destroyed is death. (1 Corinthians 15:9–26)

"For so the Lord has commanded us: 'I have set you as a light to the Gentiles, That you should be for salvation to the ends of the earth.'" Now when the Gentiles heard this, they were glad and glorified the word of the Lord. And as many as had been appointed to eternal life believed. (Acts 13:47–48)

For by grace you have been saved through faith, and that not of yourselves; it is the gift of God. (Ephesians 2:8)

For I am not ashamed of the gospel of Christ, for it is the power of God to salvation for everyone who believes, for the Jew first and also for the Greek. For in it the righteousness of God is revealed from faith to faith; as it is written, "The just shall live by faith." (Romans 1:16–17)

For when we were still without strength, in due time Christ died for the ungodly. For scarcely for a righteous man will one die; yet perhaps for a good man someone would even dare to die. But God demonstrates His own love towards us, in that while we were still sinners, Christ died for us. Much more then, having now been justified by His blood, we shall be saved from wrath through Him. (Romans 5:6–9)

No one has ascended to heaven but He who came down from heaven, that is, the Son of Man who is in heaven. And as Moses lifted up the serpent in the wilderness, even so must the Son of Man be lifted up, that whoever believes in Him should not perish but have eternal life. For God so loved the world that He gave His only begotten Son, that whoever believes in Him should not perish but have everlasting life. For God did not send His Son into the world to condemn the world, but that the world through Him might be saved. He who believes in Him is not condemned; but he who does not believe is condemned already, because he has not believed in the name of the only begotten Son of God. (John 3:13–18)

My soul, wait silently for God alone, for my expectation is from Him. He only is my rock and my salvation; He is my defense; I shall not be moved. In God is my salvation and my glory; the rock of my strength, and my refuge, is in God.

Trust in Him at all times, you people; pour out your heart before Him; God is a refuge for us. Selah. (Psalm 62:5–8)

*I am the door. If anyone enters by Me, he will be saved, and will go in and out and find pasture!* (John 10:9–11)

For if we believe that Jesus died and rose again, even so God will bring with Him those who sleep in Jesus. For this we say to you by the word of the Lord, that we who are alive and remain until the coming of the Lord will by no means precede those who are asleep. For the Lord Himself will descend from heaven with a shout, with the voice of an archangel, and with the trumpet of God. And the dead in Christ will rise first. Then we who are alive and remain shall be caught up together with them in the clouds to meet the Lord in the air. And thus we shall always be with the Lord. (1 Thessalonians 4:14–17)

For Christ did not send me to baptize, but to preach the gospel, not with wisdom of words, lest the cross of Christ should be made of no effect. For the message of the cross is foolishness to those who are perishing, but to us who are being saved it is the power of God. (1 Corinthians 1:17–18)

And this is the testimony: that God has given us eternal life, and this life is in His Son. He who has the Son has life; he who does not have the Son of God does not have life. These things I have written to you who believe in the name of the Son of God, that you may know that you have eternal life, and that you may continue to believe in the name of the Son of God. (1 John 5:11–13)

> But he who endures to end shall be saved. And this gospel of the kingdom will be preached in all the world as a witness to all the nations, and then the end will come. (Matthew 24:13–14)

I *will* love You, O Lord, my strength. The Lord is my rock and my fortress and my deliverer; My God, my strength, in whom I will trust; My shield and the horn of my salvation, my stronghold. I will call upon the Lord, who is worthy to be praised: So shall I be saved from my enemies. (Psalm 18:1–3)

Therefore He is also to save to the uttermost those who come to God through Him, since He always lives to make intercession for them. (Hebrews 7:25)

> Then Jesus said to His disciples, "If anyone desires to come after Me, let him deny himself, and take up his cross, and follow Me. For whoever desires to save his life will lose it, but whoever loses his life for My sake will find it. For what profit is it to a man if he gains the whole world, and loses his own soul? Or what will a man give in exchange for his soul? For the Son of Man will come in the glory of His Father with His angels, and then He will reward each according to his works. Assuredly, I say to you, there are some standing here who shall not taste death till they see the Son of Man coming in His kingdom." (Matthew 16:24–28)

The righteous cry out, and the Lord hears, And delivers them out of all their troubles. The Lord is near to those who have a broken heart, And saves such as have a contrite spirit. Many are the afflictions of the righteous, But the Lord delivers him out of them all. (Psalm 34:17–19)

For our citizenship is in heaven, from which we also eagerly wait for the Savior, the Lord Jesus Christ, who will transform our lowly body that it may be conformed to His glorious body, according to the working by which He is able even to subdue all things to Himself. (Philippians 3:20–21)

Heal me, O Lord, and I shall be healed; Save me, and I shall be saved, for You are my praise. (Jeremiah 17:14)

Show me Your ways, O Lord; teach me Your paths. Lead me in Your truth and teach me, for You are the God of my salvation; on You I wait all the day. (Psalm 25:4–5)

For the Lord is our Judge, the Lord is our Lawgiver, the Lord is our King; He will save us! (Isaiah 33:22)

And having been perfected, He became the author of eternal salvation to all who obey Him. (Hebrews 5:9)

Therefore lay aside all filthiness and overflow of wickedness, and receive with meekness the implanted word, which is able to save your souls. (James 1:21)

For I know that this will turn out for my deliverance through your prayer and the supply of the Spirit of Jesus Christ. (Philippians 1:19)

The Father loves the Son, and has given all things into His hand. He who believes in the Son has everlasting life; and he who does not believe the Son shall not see life, but the wrath of God abides on him. (John 3:35–36)

Giving thanks to the Father who has qualified us to be partakes of the inheritance of the saints in the light. He has delivered us from the power of darkness and conveyed us into the kingdom of the Son of His love, in whom we have redemption through His blood, the forgiveness of sins. (Colossians 1:12–14)

For even the Son of Man did not come to be served, but to serve, and to give His life a ransom for many. (Mark 10:45)

Salvation belongs to the Lord. Your blessing is upon Your people. Selah. (Psalm 3:8)

Good tree cannot bear bad fruit, nor can a bad tree bear good fruit. Every tree that does not bear good fruit is cut down and thrown into the fire. Therefore, by their fruits you will know them. Not everyone who says to me, "Lord, Lord," shall enter the kingdom of heaven, but he who does the will of My Father in heaven. Many will say to Me in that day, "Lord, Lord, have we not prophesied in Your name, cast out demons in Your name, and done many wonders in Your name?" And then I will declare to them, "I never knew you; depart from Me, you who practice lawlessness!" Therefore, whoever hears these saying of Mine, and does them, I will liken him to a wise man who built his house on the rock: and the rain descended, the floods came, and the winds blew and beat on that house; and it did not fall, for it was founded on the rock. But everyone who hears these saying of Mine, and does not do them, will be like a foolish man who built his house on the sand: and the rain descended, the floods came, and the winds blew and beat on that house; and it fell. And great was its fall. (Matthew 7:18–27)

For I know that my Redeemer lives, and He shall stand at last on the earth. (Job 19:25)

Oh, do not remember former iniquities against us! Let Your tender mercies come speedily to meet us, for we have been brought very low. Help us, O God of our salvation. For the glory of Your name; and deliver us, and provide atonement for our sins, for Your name's sake! (Psalm 79:8–9)

Restore us, O God; cause Your face to shine, and we shall be saved! (Psalm 80:3)

Restore us, O Lord God of hosts; cause Your face to shine, and we shall be saved! (Psalm 80:19)

Therefore I will look to the Lord; I will wait for the God of my salvation; My God will hear me. (Micah 7:7)

# CHAPTER 15

## THE SUMMARY OF WHY JESUS IS GOD

Jesus said to her, "Woman, why are you weeping? Whom are you seeking?" She, supposing Him to be the gardener, said to Him, "Sir, if You have carried Him away, tell me where You have laid Him, and I will take Him away." Jesus said to her, "Mary!" She turned and said to Him, "Rabboni!" (which is to say, Teacher). Jesus said to her, "Do not cling to Me, for I have not yet ascended to My Father; but go to My brethren and say to them, 'I am ascending to My Father and your Father, and to My God and your God.'" Mary Magdalene came and told the disciples that she had seen the Lord, and that He had spoken these things to her. Then, the same day at evening, being the first day of the week, when the doors were shut where the disciples were assembled, for fear of the Jews, Jesus came and stood in the midst, and said to them, "Peace be with you." When He had said this, He showed them His hands and His side. Then the disciples were glad when they saw the Lord. So Jesus said to them again, "Peace to you! As the Father has sent Me, I also send you." And when He had said this, He

> breathed on them, and said to them "Receive the Holy Spirit." (John 20:15–22)

> He must increase, but I must decrease. He who comes from above is above all; he who is of the earth is earthly and speaks of the earth. He who comes from heaven is above all. And what He has seen and heard, that He testifies; and no one receives His testimony. He who has received His testimony has certified that God is true. For He whom God has sent speaks the words of God, for God does not give the Spirit by measure. The Father loves the Son and has given all things into His hand. He who believes in the Son has everlasting life; and he who does not believe the Son shall not see life, but the wrath of God abides on him. (John 3:30–36)

Take notice that in verse 30, John the Baptist says, "I must decrease so that He (Jesus) can increase." Again, John the Baptist was a forerunner for Jesus coming as the Messiah, the Christ, the Savior of the whole world.

In verse 31, in the last part of the verse, John the Baptist tell us that Jesus is from heaven: "He said, 'He who comes from heaven's above all.'"

The most important message of these scripture passages are in verse 36, which state, "He who believes in the Son has everlasting life; and he who does not believe the Son (Jesus) shall not see life, (everlasting) but the wrath of God abide or (to remain, to continue) on him."

*Please, everyone, come to Jesus* and *be saved!* (Romans 10:9–10, 13).

> Then Saul, still breathing threats and murder against the disciples of the Lord, went to the high priest and asked letters from him to the

## JESUS IS GOD

synagogues of Damascus, so that if he found any who were of the Way, whether men or women, he might bring them bound to Jerusalem. As he journeyed he came near Damascus, and suddenly a light shone around him from heaven. Then he fell to the ground, and heard a voice saying to him, "Saul, Saul, why are you persecuting Me?" And he said, "Who are You, Lord?" Then the Lord said, "I am Jesus, whom you are persecuting. It is hard for you to kick against the goads." So he, trembling and astonished, said, "Lord, what do you want me to do?" Then the Lord said to him, "Arise and go into the city, and you will be told what you must do." And the men who journeyed with him stood speechless, hearing a voice but seeing no one.

Then Saul arose from the ground, and when his eyes were opened he saw no one. But they led him by the hand and brought him into Damascus. And he was three days without sight, and neither ate nor drank.

Now there was a certain disciple at Damascus named Ananias; and to him the Lord said in a vision, "Ananias." And he said, "Here I am, Lord." So the Lord said to him, "Arise and go to the street called Straight, and inquire at the house of Judas for one called Saul of Tarsus, for behold, he is praying. And in a vision he has seen a man named Ananias coming in and putting his hands on him, so that he might receive his sight." Then Ananias answered, "Lord, I have heard from many about this man, how much harm he has done to Your saints in Jerusalem. And here he has authority from the chief priests to bind all who call on Your name." But the Lord said to him, "Go, for he is a chosen vessel of Mine to bear My name before Gentiles, kings, and the children of Israel. For I will show him how many things he must suffer for My name's sake." And Ananias went his way and entered the house; and laying his hands on him he said, "Brother Saul, the Lord Jesus, who appeared to you on the road as you came, has sent me that you may receive your sight and be filled with the Holy Spirit." Immediately, there fell from his eyes something like scales, and he received his sight at once; and he arose and was baptized. So when he had received food, he was strengthened. Then Saul spent some days with the disciples at Damascus. Immediately, he preached the Christ in the synagogues, that He is the Son of God. (Acts 9:1–20)

"I am the Alpha and the Omega, the Beginning and the End," says the Lord, "who is and who was and who is to come, the Almighty." (Revelation 1:8)

I am the Alpha and the Omega, the First and the Last, and, what you see, write in a book and send it to the seven churches which are in Asia: to Ephesus, to Smyrna, to Philadelphia, and to Laodicea. (Revelation 1:11)

And when I saw Him, I fell at His feet as dead. But He laid His right hand on me, saying to me, "Do not be afraid; I am the First and the Last. I am He who lives, and was dead, and behold, I am alive forevermore. Amen. And I have the keys of Hades and of Death." (Revelation 1:17–18)

And behold, I'm coming quickly, and My reward is with Me, to give to every one according

## JESUS IS GOD

to his work. I am the Alpha and the Omega, the Beginning and the End, the First and the Last. (Revelation 22:12–13)

I Jesus, have sent My angel to testify to you these things in the churches. I am the Root and the Off-spring of David, the Bright and Morning Star. (Revelation 22:16)

He who testifies to these things says, "Surely I am coming quickly." Amen. Even so, come, Lord Jesus! The grace of our Lord Jesus Christ be with you all. Amen. (Revelation 22:20–21)

# CHAPTER 16

## Thank You

I want to thank everyone that took the time to read my book, *Jesus Is God: Understanding How You Get to Heaven*. I'm honored and humbled by it. I grew up going to special school because I had some difficulties learning, mainly reading and spelling. I never thought in my wildest dreams that I could ever become an author, but that just shows you the goodness of God. To take someone totally unqualified to do work for Him, in an area of many difficulties and challenges. God is *good all the time*! And *all the time* God *is good*! Thank you, Father, for using me.

The idea to write this book came from a conversation I was having with my son on good scriptures to use when witnessing the Gospel of Jesus Christ to all people, in an effort to lead them to the Lord so that they can be saved. He had some of his favorite scriptures, and so did I. After our conversation, the idea of this book came into my spirit. I had been wanting to do something for God. I tried other things that were less fulfilling, but this felt more of like a calling from God. I also created many musical pieces that I wanted to upload on social media before this book idea came to mind; however, it just didn't feel right at the time. Now that the book is complete and published, I feel more comfortable to put out the music. None of the music has lyrics, so what I did to make the public aware of Jesus Christ's salvation offer is to give each song its own title closely followed with, "Read St. John 3, whole chapter." John chapter 3 explains why salvation in Jesus Christ is very necessary and important, and it also explains what happens if we don't accept Jesus's free gift of salvation. I believe my target audience is, first of all, anyone that needs to be saved, even more specifically people in prisons, homeless shelters, juvenile facilities, or any place where a person has time to think and ask themselves, *How did I get here?* Luke 4:18–19 says,

> (Jesus speaking) The Spirit of the Lord is upon Me, because He has anointed Me to preach the gospel to the poor; He has sent Me to heal the brokenhearted, to proclaim liberty to the captives and recovery of sight to the blind, to set at liberty those who are oppressed; to proclaim the acceptable year of the Lord.

My main focus for this book is for anyone who reads it to be saved. Romans 10:9–13 says;

> That if you confess with your mouth the Lord Jesus and believe in your heart that God has raised Him from the dead, you will be saved. For with the heart one believes unto righteousness, and with the mouth confession is made unto salvation. For the Scripture says, "Whoever believes on Him will not be put to shame." For there is no distinction between Jew and Greek, for the shame Lord over all is rich to all who call upon Him. For "whoever calls on the name of the Lord shall be saved."

Father God, in Jesus's name, I pray that everyone that has read this book and even others who haven't been accepting in your offer of salvation.

Finally, here is a prayer for you to be led to Jesus and, thus, salvation. Believe it in your heart and say with your mouth,

> Dear Heavenly Father, in the name of Jesus, I do believe that Jesus Christ is the Son of God. I believe He died for me, hung on the cross for me, carried my sins for me, was put in a grave for me, rose from that grave for me. Come into my heart now, Lord Jesus. I accept You as my Savior and as the Master of my life. I repent of *all* sin I'm sorry, Lord. I accept your offer of forgiveness. Oh, I am now forgiven. Heaven is my home, and Jesus is my Lord. I'm in full fellowship, *hallelujah*! Thank You, Jesus!

Welcome to the body of Christ. I would strongly suggest that you get into a good Bible-believing church, one that teaches the Word of God from the Bible, so that you can grow and strengthen your walk with Jesus. It's a religion. You now have a relationship with your creator Jesus. Colossians 1:16–17 says,

> For by Him all things were created that are in heaven and that are on earth, visible and invisible, whether thrones or dominions or principalities or powers. All things were created through Him and for Him. And He is before all things, and in Him all things consist.

Please read your Bible daily, and also the scriptures mentioned in this book. Please look them all up and read the full context. Once again *thank you* to *all* the *readers*. Much *love*, *peace*, and *salvation*.

## ABOUT THE AUTHOR

The author, Leonard Horn, was born in the mid-'60s poor but blessed of God. He is from Detroit, Michigan. He grew up with learning difficulties and was in special classes from the fifth grade throughout junior college. He never thought in his wildest dreams that he would be an author, but that goes to show the blessing of Jesus.

www.ingramcontent.com/pod-product-compliance
Lightning Source LLC
LaVergne TN
LVHW061445150125
801237LV00025B/1170